COLLEGE PREP

for

MUSICIANS

COLLEGE PREP

FOR

MUSICIANS

A COMPREHENSIVE GUIDE FOR STUDENTS, PARENTS, TEACHERS, AND COUNSELORS

ANNIE BOSLER, DMA • DON GREENE, PhD
KATHLEEN TESAR, EdD

Published by Performance Mastery Project, Inc.
www.CollegePrepforMusicians.com

ISBN 978-0-578-42155-1
ISBN (e-book) 978-0-578-42244-2

Book cover and layout design by *the*BookDesigners
Cover and layout images © Shutterstock.com

Printed in the United States of America

First Printing, 2018

Annie would like to dedicate this book to her loving, supportive, and understanding parents, Bob and Diane Bosler.

Kathy would like to dedicate this book to her family.

Don would like to dedicate this book to all of the wonderful musicians he taught to win auditions for schools of their dreams.

Erin S. Armstrong, Copy Editor

THE AUTHOR TEAM

Drs. Annie Bosler, Kathleen Tesar, and Don Greene collaborated to write this book because all three have a passion for helping young students follow their dreams. What makes this book unique is how each author's background in music provides a different perspective. Together, they form a very complete picture of college preparation for musicians.

Annie Bosler taught at the Colburn Community School of Performing Arts for nearly a decade, working with hundreds of parents and students privately and through workshops focusing on college preparation for musicians. She has a 100% success rate of helping students get into music schools, and has French horn students in almost every major conservatory across the United States. As a private teacher and performing musician, Annie brings to the book what parents and students need to know during this crucial phase.

Peak performance psychologist Don Greene has worked with some of the world's top musicians, athletes, and performers. Don has been on the faculties of The Juilliard School, Colburn School, and New World Symphony. His specialty is helping musicians deal with nerves by using this energy to their advantage and performing their best when it counts. Don introduces powerful strategies and tools for high school students to use during the audition process.

Associate Dean for Enrollment Management at The Juilliard School, Kathleen Tesar gives insight into the admissions process from the perspective of the school. Having worked in admissions at the Colburn School, Eastman School of Music, Eastern Music Festival, and now The Juilliard School, Kathleen has admitted (and denied) thousands of students over the years. She specializes in helping students and parents understand why schools ask what they ask for and what happens behind the scenes in the world of admissions.

NOTE

• *If you are a student finding this book sometime in your senior year, do not worry. There will be information that is useful to you no matter at what stage you begin to read this book. Likewise, students who wish to pursue majors other than music performance will find much of interest here.*

• *The names of people referenced in this book have been changed to protect their identity.*

• *The authors of this book are not endorsing any particular schools. Any schools referenced herein are simply examples.*

• *The authors are not responsible for the content and maintenance of websites mentioned. Therefore, if a website link does not exist or the content of the site has changed, it is recommended to do a search for currently relevant information.*

CONTENTS

MAJORING IN MUSIC:
Starting and Persisting

1

Majoring in music. What does that mean? How does one prepare? And is it even possible to make a living with a degree in music?

This book addresses these questions and more. The desire to major in music can lead to a fulfilling career in many different areas of the music industry. Although often the first thought is that majoring in music means being an instrumental or vocal performer, the options are far wider than that.

Becoming a music major in college usually begins with instrument or voice lessons earlier in life. This chapter provides information about starting musical studies at a young age, and includes information on the value of good teachers and quality practicing. The wide variety of careers in music will be discussed in Chapter 11.

Some very young children show an interest in making music. Some parents give their children music lessons because they feel it is important to the child's growth. Some children find their way to music by themselves. No one can predict which of these students will want to make a career in music; sometimes it is not until high school that the choice is made to major in music on the college level. Regardless of how the desire to major in music develops, this chapter presents some basic points related to music study and development that can serve any student or parent.

WHAT WELL-ROUNDED MUSICAL TRAINING LOOKS LIKE

Musical training involves learning the fundamentals of playing an instrument or singing. Tied to this is the idea of musical literacy. One can sing in the shower or play piano without reading notes, but that does not make one musically literate, nor does it mean that one is using the instrument in a proper way. Some basic elements of musicality and musical literacy include:

- Ability to read music
- Ability to play in tune (intonation and centered pitch)
- Good rhythmic sense and steady time
- Ability to play across the range of the instrument (lowest notes to highest notes)
- Knowledge of scales, fingering patterns, all basic and advanced techniques on the instrument
- Beautiful tone (quality of sound)
- Ability to play with expression and musicality, with a broad dynamic range (loud and soft and in-between)

The elements listed here are learned by progressing through technical studies, études or exercises, and solo repertoire. Classes such as music theory, music history, aural skills, choir, chamber music, wind ensemble, orchestra, etc., help to improve one's fundamentals, and are excellent supplements to private lessons. Learning an additional instrument can help students better understand these fundamentals. Knowledge of piano is valuable to every musician, no matter what their primary instrument or voice type is.

TRUE STORY

Several years ago, I knew a young girl who began playing flute in her middle school band. I asked her about taking private lessons, and she replied that lessons were for students who could not learn in band. I explained that one-on-one music lessons also greatly benefit the ambitious learners. These lessons help students develop at their own pace, with the full attention of a trained professional to help them learn the fundamentals of their chosen instrument.

from Kathleen Tesar

THE IMPORTANT ROLE OF THE TEACHER

The private teacher plays a vital role in students' interest in their instrument or voice, their love for the art of music, their motivation to practice and improve, and the development of their work ethic. The instrumental or vocal teacher establishes the proper setup (bow hold, embouchure, etc.), guides the student through technical and fundamental routines, and chooses repertoire to fit the student's level, while simultaneously pushing the student always to do better. The teacher may also provide performance opportunities such as concerts and recitals. When a teacher/student fit is not right, the student may feel frustrated or unmotivated, so finding the right teacher is very important.

VOCABULARY: LESSONS

PRIVATE LESSONS: individualized one-on-one instruction in playing an instrument or singing

SEMI-PRIVATE LESSONS: typically means two students taking lessons together on a regular basis

GROUP LESSONS OR CLASS INSTRUCTION: an instrument or vocal technique is taught to several students at the same time

In each type of instruction, the student is taught how to play or sing. The teacher knows how to play the instrument and is passing that skill on to the student.

When choosing a private teacher, it is important to ask these questions:

Do you specialize in certain age groups or fundamental skills?
- There is a difference between training a six-year-old beginner and training a sixteen-year-old who is on the path to a career in music.

- Students who are "set up" correctly at the start of their musical studies have an advantage over students who have to spend months and years correcting improperly taught fundamentals.

Weekly lessons are the norm. How long do you think weekly lessons should be, at least to start?
- Young students may have a 30-minute lesson each week. As they get older the time may increase to 60 minutes. (The standard lesson offered in college for majors is either 50 or 60 minutes once a week.)

Do you provide performance opportunities for your students?
- Some teachers hold weekly performance classes in addition to the lessons, or arrange recitals of their students.

If there are weekly group or performance classes, may I attend one before enrolling in lessons, or can you put me in touch with current students and/or parents?

- It is helpful to learn how the teacher's current students are performing and how they enjoy lessons.

When the student is older and showing an interest in making a career in music, these questions are important:

Have you helped any of your students apply to college, as music majors or otherwise?

- Where were those students accepted?

- Where are they now?

- Are any of them making a living as musicians?

Do you help your students find and choose instruments when needed?

- A poor instrument can prevent a student from consistently progressing.

Do you help your students make prescreening and audition recordings?

Do you help with all aspects of the supplemental application for non-music majors?

It is a normal part of musical development for a student to need different teachers or vocal coaches at different stages of study. It is rare to find one teacher or coach with whom a student should spend all of their time from elementary to middle school to high school. Parents should make sure that their children make the move to a new teacher or coach at the right point.

CHANGING TEACHERS

One ethical point regarding changing teachers: If a change of teacher is to be made, it is best for all parties to be open about the change. Never start taking lessons with another teacher or coach without consulting the primary mentor first.

There are situations where a student may have a primary teacher, and see another teacher to fix certain problems. Parents must make sure that the teachers are aware of each other so that their teaching does not conflict. This is not the same thing as working with the teacher's assistant, or going off to summer camp, where the student will have another teacher for a short period. In the first case, a teaching assistant is subordinate to the primary teacher, and works under the primary teacher's direction. In the second case, the choice of summer camp is usually made together with the primary teacher.

SUSTAINING THE LOVE OF MUSIC

Once a student starts studying an instrument or singing, the pressure of constantly improving or having a great performance sometimes consumes them or their parents. Occasionally the temptation can arise to attempt music for which one is not yet ready. This is why one needs an experienced teacher who can pace the student's development appropriately. Even more importantly, the right teacher will keep the student's joy alive. This is especially important during the challenging college application process.

QUALITY PRACTICING: LEARNING A SKILL FOR LIFE

Improvement is directly proportional to practice time. However, pushing students to practice can be detrimental to their love of music. One question parents often ask is, "How much should my child be practicing?" The answer is not in minutes or hours, but in the *quality* of the practice. Five minutes of dedicated, focused practice is more effective than thirty minutes of vague, unfocused practice. Students with immense natural talent who do not work hard will at some point be surpassed by students who work harder and smarter.

DIG DEEPER: PRACTICE HABITS

In the book *Outliers*, author Malcolm Gladwell drew on the research of Dr. K. Anders Ericsson (a psychologist who studies expertise) to create the "10,000-hour rule": A student who starts putting in long hours of quality practice early in life will have accumulated more hours than someone who starts later. Such a lead can never be made up. However, if the student who starts later works harder and smarter, they may achieve more than the student who started earlier but did not invest the attention and energy needed for intelligent practicing.

Remember: Intelligent practicing is never about the clock. Check out this TED-Ed video by authors Annie Bosler and Don Greene: *How to practice...for just about anything* https://ed.ted.com/lessons/how-to-practice-effectively-for-just-about-anything-annie-bosler-and-don-greene.

Slow practice in the early stages of learning new material is absolutely crucial to a successful performance. When the brain is learning something new, it maps neural pathways to retrieve this information. If material is not learned slowly and efficiently, the pathway is not paved in a clear and direct route. This makes the information more difficult to retrieve, especially under pressure. Students should not hurry the process of getting from their slowest tempo up to the performance tempo—in other words, don't speed up the metronome too soon.

HOW THE BRAIN ABSORBS NEW INFORMATION

Quiet, focused practice makes it easier for the brain to retrieve information it has stored. Students who practice while watching TV, for example, are multitasking. Multitasking can cause new information to go to the wrong part of the brain and can make accessing this information difficult. Without distractions, the information goes to the part of the brain where it is easily retrievable.

Neuroscientist Russell Poldrack studies the brain and multitasking. His interview explains how learning while multitasking differs from learning while focused on a single task: http://projectinfolit.org/smart-talks/item/109-russell-poldrack.

Taking breaks is important for the practice routine. Since most instruments are asymmetrical and are required to be held for long periods of time, breaks give the body a chance to rest physically. Breaks also allow the mind to rest so it can resume a particular task with a better ability to focus.

As a student progresses and the technical and musical demands increase, the student must develop more sophisticated practice strategies. Here are some examples:

- Make a plan: Before starting the practice session, map out what will be practiced, when it will be practiced, how long the practice session will last, and what the desired result is. Make sure to schedule breaks as well.

- Keep a practice log: After practicing, write down the length of the practice session, the time of day, what was practiced, and the results. This will help in understanding practice habits and problem areas.

- Practice with a metronome. If possible, practice counting out loud while you play. (This obviously will not work for singers or wind instrumentalists.)

- Practice for 45 minutes, take a 15-minute break, repeat. Longer practice blocks require a detailed practice plan.

- Practice for one hour, take a break for one hour, repeat. Longer practice blocks require a detailed practice plan.

- Practice many times a day for 5-10 minutes each time, addressing a clearly stated goal each time.

- Practice for one minute, break for one minute, practice for one minute, etc., for 30 minutes; then take a longer break. Repeat many times a day. This is an especially good strategy when preparing for auditions, where an applicant may be asked to start and stop playing several times.

- Choose a set number of minutes to practice each goal. Use a timer to track the number of minutes; once it beeps, you are finished.

RESILIENCE

One trait that all musicians must cultivate is resilience—the ability to bounce back and recover from adversity. Resilience is part of persisting toward and achieving a goal. Many successful musicians have lost far more auditions and competitions than they have won. In other words, they have failed numerous times and bounced back. The resilient musician uses every unsuccessful attempt to identify ways to improve.

Music students or their parents may turn down an opportunity to audition or perform because the "repertoire is not ready" or "it may not go well." Assuming the opportunity is reasonable (that is, the student is not trying to enter a major competition after only several months of serious study), embrace the experience. Afterwards, work with the teacher to analyze the strengths and weaknesses of the performance and determine the steps to make things better the next time.

AN INSPIRATIONAL STORY FOR PARENTS

Sara Blakely, American billionaire businesswoman, shares one of the secrets to success. Her father asked her the same question each night at dinner, "What have you failed at this week?" Her father encouraged her to fail. The lesson Sara's father was teaching her is that the only failure is not trying. Visit: http://www.cnbc.com/2013/10/16/billionaire-sara-blakely-says-secret-to-success-is-failure.html.

A GENERAL TIMELINE FOR HIGH SCHOOL STUDENTS WHO WANT TO MAJOR IN MUSIC

2

The following timeline can be a useful tool for prospective music majors. It starts in the freshman and sophomore years of high school, when a student should be preparing in a broad sense, and then focuses on the necessary steps a junior and senior should take when applying to music schools. The busiest semesters for someone planning to major in music will be the spring of junior year and both semesters of senior year.

The lists below are addressed to students, who need to become very familiar with the information. However, since parents, teachers, and school counselors all play a supporting role in helping students stay on track, everyone is encouraged to read them.

FRESHMAN AND SOPHOMORE YEARS

- Study with a teacher or voice coach who has a track record of getting students into good music schools and who will push you musically and technically.

- Discuss with your teacher the pieces appropriate to learn at this stage to cover standard repertoire. Make sure that you are working on solos, etudes, excerpts, fundamentals, and sight-reading.

- Develop thorough, consistent practice habits. Some students find it helpful to keep a practice log or journal. There are many ways to do this; the best one is the one that fits you. Make sure your practice plan includes both short-term and long-term goals.

- Perform as often as possible, and as often as your teacher recommends, in places including:
    - Studio classes
    - Solo recitals
    - Nursing homes
    - Churches
    - Gatherings of family and friends

- Enroll in:
    - Local youth orchestras, wind ensembles, or choirs
    - Local youth chamber music programs

- Consider applying to:
    - Summer programs and festivals (Most applications are due between November 1 and April 15, depending on the program.)
    - Local concerto or solo competitions
    - State/regional honors orchestra, band, and choir programs

- Start having conversations with your parents, teachers, and school counselors about applying to music schools as your interest develops.

- Speak with your high school counselor about your course load. The goal is to plan ahead in order to have a senior year schedule that leaves ample room to focus on college auditions.

- Begin compiling a list of colleges where your friends from orchestra, band, choir, or summer programs are applying. Speak with the seniors and ask them where they are applying and why they chose those schools.

- Contact prospective teachers and coaches, and set up introductory lessons whenever possible (see Appendix 1).

- Check local concert schedules to see if great teachers, performers, orchestras, or ensembles will be in your area. Whenever possible, attend these masterclasses, operas, or concerts.

JUNIOR YEAR

- Start asking yourself these questions:

    ○ What school(s) would I like to attend?

    ○ Do I want to stay close to home or go further away?

    ○ Do I want to be a music major? A music minor? Something else, but still take lessons or play in the marching band?

    ○ Do I want to double major (two areas of music study) or pursue two degrees (music and something non-music)?

    ○ With whom would I like to study?

    ○ In what part of the country would I like to live?

    ○ Do I want to go to a big school or a small school?

- Do I want to go to a conservatory, a "traditional" university, or a music school within a university?

- Do I want a school that specializes in a certain area of music (education, performance, film composing, audio engineering, etc.)?

- Make arrangements to visit schools and tour their campuses (see Appendix 2).

  - Plan ahead: Many schools have scheduled campus tour times; in some cases you must have a reservation for a tour. An introductory lesson with the instrumental professor or voice teacher would need to be arranged first before scheduling the tour. Make sure to schedule the lesson several weeks in advance of your visit. Do not expect the teacher to be available if you have not contacted him or her ahead of time.

- Begin looking for scholarships. There are many scholarships for college that are open only to juniors in high school.

- Consider applying to:

  - Summer programs and festivals (Most applications are due between November 1 and April 15, depending on the program.)

  - Local concerto or solo competitions

  - State and local honors orchestra, band, and choir programs

- Spring: Determine your college audition repertoire. Start learning and performing it.

- Summer: Perform college audition repertoire as much as possible. Finish college/university trips, tours, and lessons. Begin to work on the essays/personal statements for each school. Summer festivals, internships, volunteer work, etc., are recommended to strengthen your application.

SENIOR YEAR

Note: This timeline may be different if you are: a high school student wishing to apply for school outside of the United States, an undergraduate student wishing to transfer schools, or an undergraduate student wishing to apply to graduate programs.

- August through September: If you have not done this already, finish college/university trips, tours, and lessons. Continue to polish and perform your audition repertoire.

- October through November: Make prescreening recordings.

- October 1: Applications for FAFSA (Free Application for Federal Student Aid) are available. http://www.fafsa.ed.gov/

  - FAFSA is the gateway application for all federal funding as well as some college scholarships and grants.

  - In addition to the FAFSA website, the U.S. government has lots of solid information about aid (including grants and loans) at https://studentaid.ed.gov/sa/.

  - Pay attention to deadlines for other types of aid including institutional aid.

  - Search for private scholarships through websites such as these (and continue searching, there are many more):

    - Cappex.com
    - Collegeboard.org
    - Collegenet.com
    - Fastweb.com
    - Scholarshipmonkey.com
    - Scholarships.com

  - Never, ever, pay to get scholarship information—it is available for free. See Chapter 10 for more information about financial aid and scholarships.

- December 1: The most common music conservatory deadline for applying and submitting prescreening recordings.

- December through January: Most, if not all applications and pre-screening recordings are due. Make sure to pay close attention to each school's deadline.

- January through March: College/university auditions take place. This is the time to prepare and perform your mock auditions before the real ones.

- January through April: Check with your home state for financial aid programs administered by the state. (For instance, March 2 is the deadline for California residents to apply for the Cal Grant, the largest source of California state-funded student financial aid.)

- March 2: FAFSA application closes.

- April 1: Applicants are notified of decisions for admission and financial aid. Study and compare the financial aid offers with the help of a counselor and parents. (Some schools send out admissions decisions on a rolling basis, but these are generally not selective music schools.)

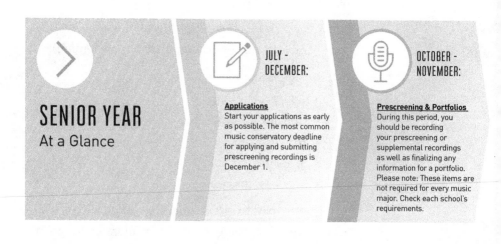

SENIOR YEAR
At a Glance

JULY – DECEMBER:

Applications
Start your applications as early as possible. The most common music conservatory deadline for applying and submitting prescreening recordings is December 1.

OCTOBER – NOVEMBER:

Prescreening & Portfolios
During this period, you should be recording your prescreening or supplemental recordings as well as finalizing any information for a portfolio. Please note: These items are not required for every music major. Check each school's requirements.

- April 1 - 30: This is the window to negotiate financial aid packages. (Note that not all schools negotiate.)

- May 1: Deadline for applicants to accept or decline an offer of admission. Make sure to send an email or letter to all of the teachers whom you have had to turn down, as well as sending in your enroll/decline forms.

- May/June: Follow through on any housing deposits, health insurance (find out if your parents are covering you, otherwise you will need the school insurance), and any required remedial summer classes (math, English, etc.)

- June/July: Send a final transcript to the school you will be attending. (Check the school's deadline for the transcript.)

- Summer: Summer festivals, college summer bridge programs, internships, etc. are a great way to spend the summer after the senior year. If needed, take a piano class or an introduction to music theory.

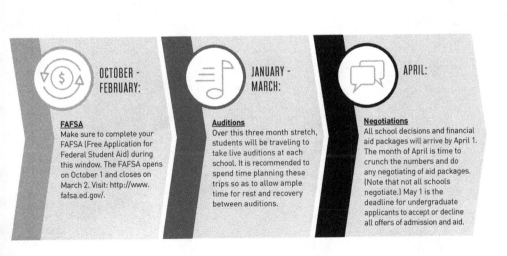

OCTOBER - FEBRUARY:

FAFSA
Make sure to complete your FAFSA (Free Application for Federal Student Aid) during this window. The FAFSA opens on October 1 and closes on March 2. Visit: http://www.fafsa.ed.gov/.

JANUARY - MARCH:

Auditions
Over this three month stretch, students will be traveling to take live auditions at each school. It is recommended to spend time planning these trips so as to allow ample time for rest and recovery between auditions.

APRIL:

Negotiations
All school decisions and financial aid packages will arrive by April 1. The month of April is time to crunch the numbers and do any negotiating of aid packages. (Note that not all schools negotiate.) May 1 is the deadline for undergraduate applicants to accept or decline all offers of admission and aid.

UNDERSTANDING SCHOOLS AND MUSIC DEGREES

3

In order to make wise choices about where to apply as a music major, it is helpful to understand the basic underlying structures. The most important things to consider are the types of institutions, degrees, and majors. At the post-secondary (university) level, music students have a different relation to these three structures than non-music students. An understanding of these differences can help with deciding where to apply. Note that the following examples are just that: examples. They are meant to illustrate the wide range of options available. Remember that the "right" school is always the one where the student thrives and learns.

TYPES OF INSTITUTIONS

Universities tend to be large, diverse institutions, made up of different colleges or schools (for example, one university might include a business college, a music school, and a medical college). A music student in a university is required to take the General Education (sometimes called "GenEd" or "G.E.") curriculum that all university students must take. A music major may sit in GenEd classes next to a pre-law student, while rooming with a business major, and complete enough classes to earn a minor in French. At a university, it is very possible to combine different degrees, majors, and minors.

EXAMPLES:

- Bienen School of Music (Northwestern University)
- Frost School of Music (University of Miami)
- Jacobs School of Music (Indiana University)
- Shepherd School of Music (Rice University)
- Thornton School of Music (University of Southern California)

A **conservatory** is typically small, independent (that is, not part of a university), and focused completely on the art form. A music student may sit in core liberal arts classes next to a composition major, room with a jazz major, and complete enough classes to earn a minor in music theory, but that student won't enjoy the diversity of non-music choices available at a university. They also will not have a football team or the same clubs and activities found in universities.

EXAMPLES:

- Berklee College of Music (Massachusetts)
- Boston Conservatory at Berklee (Massachusetts)
- Cleveland Institute of Music (Ohio)
- Colburn School Conservatory of Music (California)
- Cornish College of the Arts (Washington)
- Curtis Institute (Pennsylvania)

- The Juilliard School (New York)
- Manhattan School of Music (New York)
- New England Conservatory (Massachusetts)
- San Francisco Conservatory (California)

One variation that combines some characteristics of both of these is the **conservatory within a university**. In this setting, a student has access to all of the university but the music curriculum is structured like that of a conservatory.

EXAMPLES:

- The Bob Cole Conservatory at California State University, Long Beach (California)
- Lynn University Conservatory of Music (Florida)
- Eastman School of Music, University of Rochester (New York)
- Peabody Institute of The Johns Hopkins University (Maryland)

A **college** falls between a university and conservatory in size and focus. Typically, a college will have a department of music, rather than an entire school of music.

EXAMPLES:

- Hunter College Music Department (New York)
- Reed College Music Department (Oregon)
- Spelman College Department of Music (Georgia)
- William Jewell College Department of Music (Missouri)

AGREEMENTS BETWEEN CONSERVATORIES AND OTHER POST-SECONDARY INSTITUTIONS

Some independent conservatories have legal agreements that allow conservatory students to enroll simultaneously at another post-secondary institution for a non-music program, degree, major, or minor. These arrangements are very specific and individual, and may require application and admission to both institutions.

Examples of agreements between conservatories and universities:

- Barnard-Juilliard and Columbia-Juilliard Cross-Registration
- Cleveland Institute of Music-Case Western Reserve University Joint Music Program
- New England Conservatory-Tufts University

There are many variations on arrangements between schools, including the terms used to describe programs and the actual program parameters. Students are advised to do their research carefully!

TYPES OF DEGREE PROGRAMS

Options for degrees following high school are:

- Undergraduate degrees: bachelor's degrees
- Graduate degrees: master's degrees

- Post-graduate degrees: doctoral degrees
- Certificates and diplomas: non-degree granting programs at various post-secondary levels; upon completion, one is awarded a certificate or a diploma (but not a bachelor's, master's, or doctoral degree)

UNDERGRADUATE DEGREES

Here is a list of common undergraduate degrees for music majors:

- Bachelor of Music (BM)
- Bachelor of Fine Arts (BFA)
- Bachelor of Arts (BA)
- Bachelor of Science (BS)

There are other undergraduate degrees, but these four degrees are the ones most likely to be of interest to music students. The differences between one degree and another can be found in the name of the degree, the course requirements, the focus area in which the curriculum is based, and how the school wishes to present the degree. Oftentimes curricula from two different schools will be similar but the degrees will be titled differently. This is why one must research beyond just the degree titles in order to find the right match between student and program.

DIG DEEPER: DEGREE STANDARDS

The National Association of Schools of Music (NASM) requires member institutions to adhere to the standards spelled out in its Handbook. The current Handbook, together with updates, can be found at this website: http://nasm.arts-accredit.org/index.jsp?page=Standards-Handbook.

The **Bachelor of Music** (BM) degree is the standard undergraduate degree offered in conservatories and schools of music within universities. ("BMus" is sometimes used instead of "BM.") NASM, which accredits music programs, calls the BM degree a "professional" degree, requiring at least 65% music content. (*NASM Handbook 2017-18, page 87.*) Students in BM programs choose a branch of music in which to major; the choice of major drives the application and admission process. Examples of BM degrees include: "BM in Applied Music (Performance)," "BM in Composition," "BM in Jazz Studies & Contemporary Media," "BM in Music Education," "BM in Music Theory," etc.

The BFA degree is the **Bachelor of Fine Arts** degree. This degree is also a professional degree, like the BM degree, but is more typically offered in the visual arts, dance, or theatre, rather than in music. The majority of the course requirements in a BFA program consist of a performance component (lessons, ensembles, performance classes, etc.). Usually the curriculum is based on the ratio of two-third studies in music and one-third studies in general liberal arts classes. There is often an area of study specified within a BFA such as a "BFA in Music" or a "BFA in Art," and within a "BFA in Music" students may have an instrumental subset such as a "BFA in Music with an emphasis in horn performance."

Many people are familiar with the designation "BA," which refers to the **Bachelor of Arts** degree. The BA is offered in many colleges and universities. This is a liberal arts degree, which means there is a focus on the humanities (in contrast with a Bachelor of Science degree, which focuses on science). The curriculum of a BA degree has only about 30-45% music content; in other words, the weight of a BA degree is towards studies *other than* music. For this reason, the BA is a good choice for those who want a broader education in the humanities, but with the ability to include a solid amount of music study. Students interested in music history, music criticism, or music journalism in particular benefit from BA studies.

While the BA degree emphasizes the liberal arts, the **Bachelor of Science** (BS) degree has more of an emphasis on technical or scientific studies. The BS degree is not typical in performance-based music studies, but may be an appropriate course of study for a student interested in music recording technology, music business, audio engineering, or other such topics. That said, even though the emphasis may be on non-performance majors (recording, business, etc.), the curriculum may slant towards performance (live recording, composition) or it may slant towards science (physics, electronics, acoustics, etc.). When looking at a BS degree, students should examine the curriculum to see what the emphasis is and to determine how their interests are best served. Note that the schools where the BS curriculum is performance-based usually require an audition.

DIG DEEPER: DEGREE REQUIREMENTS

Prospective students can find a lot of information about a school by visiting the school's website. To find more specific details about degrees, look under the "current students" part of the website for the actual semester-by-semester requirements. A great example of this is the University of Michigan's School of Music, Theatre and Dance. This page: http://www.music.umich.edu/current_students/student_resources/curricularlayouts.htm shows the various undergraduate degrees and how the requirements differ between them. For example, contrast the BM in Voice Performance (what they call "BMus") with the BFA in Musical Theatre to see how the requirements change along with the focus of the program. There are similar listings on conservatory websites, such as this page on the Peabody Institute website: https://peabody.jhu.edu/academics/instruments-areas-of-study/.

When all is said and done, the "right" degree is the one that teaches the student what the student wants to learn. A student who wants to be a composer needs to learn the tools of composition. It doesn't matter if that is in a BA program or a BM program. Five years after graduation, the thing that will matter the most is whether the student can compose. On the other hand, if that composition major really wants to compose music for video games, then the best degree program is going to be one that not only teaches composition but also gives the student familiarity with the world of video game design and what it demands of a composer—and that can happen in a BA program, a BM program, a BS program, or a BFA program.

Research, research, research everything possible about the degree programs at the schools in which the student is most interested.

GRADUATE AND POST-GRADUATE DEGREES

The **Master of Music** (MM) degree and the **Master of Arts** (MA) degree are both two-year graduate (post-baccalaureate) degrees. As with all post-baccalaureate programs, the requirement for general education courses falls away; program content focuses intensely on the student's major. The MM, like the BM, is slanted towards applied learning: students will spend most of their time performing, composing, etc. A student in an MA program will spend more time researching and writing.

Following study at the master's level, music students typically have two choices of doctoral degrees. The **Doctor of Musical Arts** (DMA) degree is the professional degree; the **Doctor of Philosophy** (PhD) degree is the research degree. When looking at doctoral degree programs, make sure to study the curriculum. Some doctoral degree programs are intensely academic, requiring a dissertation, while others are more performance based and include lecture recitals and minor fields.

CERTIFICATE AND DIPLOMA PROGRAMS: WHEN COLLEGE DOES NOT LEAD TO A DEGREE

It pays to mention, especially for students in the performing arts, that one does not always have to earn a degree. However, the choice to complete a certificate or diploma program instead of a degree program has consequences that should be understood before beginning such a program.

Non-degree programs offered by universities, colleges, and conservatories are still accredited (assuming the institution is accredited), but they are not degrees. This means they focus on training, not on general education or research. The programs may be offered on the undergraduate level, but are more typically offered on the graduate level. Here are some titles:

- Artist Certificate

- Artist Diploma

- Diploma

- Graduate Certificate

- Graduate Diploma

- Graduate Performance Diploma

- Performance Diploma

- Performer's Certificate

- Professional Certificate

- Professional Studies Certificate

There is far less standardization of requirements in these programs than in degree programs. For example, a bachelor's degree typically requires completion of 120 credits. Certificates and diplomas are defined by the institution, in length and in number of credits; there is no standard number of credits required for these programs.

Non-degree progams are a good choice for an advanced student who is already building a career (for example, has concert commitments or a heavy competition schedule), or for a student who wants the musical training without the academics, or even for a student whose English language skills are not strong enough for a degree program.

CAUTION: To enroll in a bachelor's degree program, an applicant must have completed high school (or its equivalent). To enroll in a master's degree program, an applicant must have completed a bachelor's degree. To enroll in a doctoral program, an applicant must have completed a master's degree. A non-degree program cannot take the place of a degree program within that hierarchy.

WHY GET A DEGREE IF A NON-DEGREE PROGRAM IS SHORTER (AND CHEAPER)? HERE'S WHY:

A degree is a degree—once a student has a bachelor's degree, forever after they have a bachelor's degree. If a student earns a Bachelor of Music degree in flute performance, and then is injured and can no longer play, that student still has a path into graduate school.

Working through a four-year undergraduate degree program— managing one's time, setting goals, meeting deadlines, learning responsibility—is great preparation for life and supporting oneself as an adult, no matter what the degree program.

TYPES OF MAJORS

...erstanding of the available choices in majors is important ...he school's decision whether to admit a particular student will ...epend on how the student is evaluated in that major.

...er words, if an applicant who plays piano wants to major in clas-...o performance, then the weight of the admission decision ...t and foremost on how well the applicant plays piano. If that same ...cant plays piano but wants to major in composition, then the weight of the admission decision will be on the applicant's compositions, and not so much on how well the applicant plays the piano.

In the music world, students choose a school because of their desire to pursue a specific major at that school. All of their preparation is directed towards being acceptable in that major. Here are some options for music majors:

- Composition
- Conducting
- Film Scoring
- Jazz Studies
- Music Business
- Music Education
- Music Entertainment
- Music Industry
- Music Ministry
- Music Production
- Music Technology

- Music Theory

- Music Therapy

- Musicology

- Performance

- Popular Music

- Songwriting

Appendix 3 lists undergraduate degree programs and majors, highlighting the wide array of options. Other programs may exist that are not included here, and who knows what may be created in the future. Note, however, that on the undergraduate (post-secondary) level, there are fewer *degrees*, but more variations in *majors*. On the graduate (master, doctor, post-baccalaureate) levels, the degree specifies the focus.

DIG DEEPER: APPLICATION REQUIREMENTS

Here is one example of how a student's choice of major changes the requirements to apply:

- University of Southern California Thornton School of Music: http://music.usc.edu/admission/appreqs/

DOUBLING UP

Usually, somewhere in the discussion about schools and majors, the question of double majors and double (dual) degrees comes up. There is quite a bit of confusion about the two terms.

It may be possible at some schools to complete two majors within the same degree program. This is called a **double major**. For example, jazz performance and music education are two majors that can be pursued at the same time at some schools; the student then graduates with one music degree that lists two majors.

A student who has applied to and been accepted to two degree programs at the same institution is doing what is called a **double degree**. An example of this is a student enrolled in a Bachelor of Music degree and a Bachelor of Science degree. The coursework for both degrees is completed simultaneously.

To state the obvious, the applicant should be aware that a double major or double degree will require a heavier course load and additional semesters to complete.

A FEW EXAMPLES OF DOUBLING UP

Eastman School of Music of the University of Rochester has a very clear description of the dual degree: http://www.esm.rochester.edu/academic-affairs/esmstudents/dual-degree-program/dual-degree/.

Here is Oberlin's description of their double degree program: https://www.oberlin.edu/admissions-and-aid/double-degree-program. At both Oberlin and Eastman, admission to each degree proceeds independently of the other, with separate applications and separate approvals.

Beinen School of Music at Northwestern University offers several different five-year undergraduate degrees. These combine music and liberal arts, music and journalism, or music and engineering. They also offer double majors within the School of Music or between the School of Music and other schools within the university. It is clearly pointed out that a double major takes four years, but a dual degree takes five: https://www.music.northwestern.edu/academics/dual.

Bard Conservatory is unique among these schools because all undergraduates are required to pursue five-year double-degree programs: http://www.bard.edu/conservatory/undergraduate/.

Why double up when one major or degree can be challenging enough? In the best scenario, a student will complete a double degree or a double major because they are passionate about two different things, and can envision a future in which both choices come into play. Think about this example: An undergraduate classical voice major dreams of studying opera in Vienna. She completes a BM in voice performance and a BA in German. Now she is prepared for the next step in her career. Or imagine a jazz major who loves teaching teenagers. He completes a BM degree with majors in jazz performance and music education, in anticipation of a career teaching high school jazz band, while playing in his own professional jazz combo. Both of these students have taken advantage of doubling in the best way possible.

In the worst scenario, a student will seek a double major or double degree because of fear (sometimes their own fear, sometimes their parents' fear) —the fear that they will not be able to make a living as a musician. A parent or school counselor may suggest that it is only wise to go into music with a "Plan B". However, there is a compelling argument against studying outside of one's major in music, and that is the idea that in order to succeed in music, one needs to be committed 110%. If the student has to subtract time away from practicing in order to write a paper, then the applied teacher will be very unhappy. And to be honest, the applied teacher may not be wrong.

Some applied teachers state, "If you feel you need a backup, you do." In other words, the student has already created a situation in which a backup is needed by watering down their commitment of time and energy. The skills that a music student learns and some of the career options available will be discussed later. But to put it bluntly, if a student is afraid to go into music because they might not be able to make a living, *they should not go into music.* Without passion to sustain them through the inevitable challenges, it will simply be a bad career choice.

MINORS

A student does not apply to a minor as part of the process of applying to a school. The term "minor" refers to credit hours: If enough courses (credits) are completed in a specific area, the student then earns a minor. A college minor can be strategic. An example of this would be a voice performance major who minors in German (instead of doing a full double degree) because the student is planning to study in Germany for graduate school. One can also earn a minor in music if they choose to major in something else.

If a student is not planning on majoring in music, but wants to continue studying in some fashion (for example, taking lessons, singing in a choir, studying arranging), it does make sense to investigate a school's policies and offerings before enrolling. Sometimes there can be an advantage to expressing an interest in music while applying. (For example, if the school orchestra needs more viola players and the student plays viola, that may be an opportunity for scholarship support.) In general, when the student is applying to major in music, the question of minors comes later.

DECIDING WHERE TO APPLY:
Lists and Strategies

4

There are hundreds of options for post-secondary education, both in music and outside of music. In fact, there are so many choices of schools it can become overwhelming (see Appendix 3). This chapter describes how to strategically create a list of schools. The list might start with twenty to thirty schools, and then be narrowed down to ten schools or less. This number will vary depending on the applicant's instrumental or vocal speciality, and major area within music (theory, performance, arranging, etc.).

STARTING A LIST

Each applicant will approach how they make their list of schools in a different way, using different tools. A high school student (or a non-musician parent) may feel that they don't know where to begin the search for music schools. The first tool is the student's network—people they already know:

- The student's applied (private instrument or voice) teacher
- The student's orchestra, band, or choir director, or ensemble coach
- The student's peers who are also applying or who have applied to college in recent years
- Fellow students at music festivals, summer camps, solo and ensemble contests, and regional, state, or all-city orchestras, bands, and choirs
- Other parents, especially those of musical children
- School counselors and independent consultants

These people may provide ideas about schools that the applicant has not considered or that are perhaps unfamiliar. The names of all the schools these people suggest should be added to the applicant's list. Don't worry if the list of schools is long; it will be narrowed down.

RESEARCH

- Search the internet for favorite performers: What school did this musician attend? With whom did they study? (This information is usually found in the musician's biography.)
- Check out the school websites: university websites, music conservatory websites, or music department websites. Try to get a feel for the school through the website.
- College search websites can also come in handy. Here are some general examples:
  - Big Future: https://bigfuture.collegeboard.org/
  - Chegg: https://www.chegg.com/schools/
  - College Insight: http://college-insight.org/
  - Peterson's: https://www.petersons.com/

- These are college search websites through the U.S. government:
  - College Navigator: https://nces.ed.gov/collegenavigator/
  - College Scorecard: https://collegescorecard.ed.gov/

ASKING THE RIGHT QUESTIONS

GENERAL QUESTIONS FOR ALL COLLEGE APPLICANTS TO ASK THEMSELVES

These questions are valid whether the student is a music applicant or not:

1. Do I want to go to a large school or a small school?
2. Do I want to go to school close to home or far away from home?
3. Do I want to be part of a large student body or a small student body?
4. Do I want to be able to elect classes outside my chosen field?
5. Is the "college experience" (meaning college sports, Greek life, clubs, etc.) important to me or not?
6. Do I prefer a certain type of weather?
7. Do I enjoy watching the seasons change?

SPECIFIC QUESTIONS FOR THE MUSIC MAJOR APPLICANT

Here are some key questions that a music applicant should think about:

1. What major do I intend to study?
2. What type of school am I looking for—a music conservatory, university/college, conservatory within a university, or a conservatory that has an agreement with another post-secondary institution?
3. Do I want a curriculum focused on music, or a curriculum with broader general education choices?

4. Do I want to have the option of adding majors and minors outside of music?

5. If I have identified a school, do I know the teacher(s) in my intended major?

6. If I have identified a teacher, do I know where they teach?

QUESTIONS RELATED TO MUSIC STUDY

1. Is the music curriculum thorough, covering music theory, music history, aural skills, and keyboard skills, as well as performance classes such as orchestra and chamber music?

2. Have I compared curricula between schools? How many core academic/general education classes will I have to take at each school? What kinds of classes are available, including classes outside of music?

3. What is the practice room situation? How many practice rooms are there? Where are they located? Are they in the dorms? What hours are they available?

4. What orchestral playing opportunities are available for freshmen? (This is particularly important for winds, brass, and percussion players.) Are non-string players assigned to an orchestra as freshmen?

5. If I have taken AP classes, will I get credit for them? (Typically, AP Music Theory classes help with theory placement, but will not substitute for actual classes. In addition, some music schools may not accept AP classes or only take a few credits. It is important to learn if the schools in which you are interested take AP credits before overloading a high school schedule with AP courses.)

6. Does the school have a scholarship specifically for undergraduate music majors? If so, what is the application process and deadline?

7.   What are graduates of this program/department/school doing? (This question can be directed toward the applied professor and current students. If necessary, contact the alumni office for information about recent graduates.)

VOCABULARY: APPLIED STUDIES AND STUDIOS

In music schools, the hands-on study of one's instrument or voice is referred to as **APPLIED STUDIES**. The teacher who gives the weekly one-on-one lessons is called the **APPLIED TEACHER**. That teacher usually has a group of students to whom they give weekly lessons. Together, that group is called a **STUDIO** and often become the student's closest cohort. This term **STUDIO** is also used to describe the teacher's physical teaching space. Some applied teachers have all of the students meet together for a weekly **STUDIO CLASS**.

You will hear these terms used frequently; for example: *Who is your top choice for applied teacher? Who else is in that studio? How many credits do you earn for applied studies?*

HOW DOES A STUDENT FIND AN APPROPRIATE APPLIED TEACHER?

This question should be part of the college search, especially for performance majors. Here are suggested approaches:

- Think of the search for an applied teacher as an expanding spiral. The starting point is the student's current teacher. With whom did this musician study? Who was their primary teacher? Who else did their primary teacher train? Identify where these people are teaching now.

- Look at the student's peers. With whom do they study now, and with whom did their teachers study? Identify where they are teaching now.

- Answer the questions listed earlier in this chapter to identify preferred types of schools, then search their faculty list to find out who are the applied teachers there.

- Use the inverse approach: create a list of teachers by using the network, then search to find the schools where they teach.

- The applicant can look at famous teachers and ask who were some of their students, and where do those former students teach or perform? The competition for a place in the studio of a well-known teacher can be fierce, but some of their graduates may be fine teachers themselves.

Once applicants have used these approaches to identify applied teachers of interest, the school with which those teachers are associated should be added to the applicant's list of possible schools.

THE IMPORTANCE OF THE APPLIED TEACHER

For performance majors, there is nothing more important than the applied teacher. Four years of study with an applied teacher helps the student solidify technique, develop an understanding of the repertoire for their instrument or voice type, and build performance skills and artistry. The student also observes all of these things happening with their peers in the same studio which can serve as a powerful motivator and greatly influence a student's own progress. The applied teacher is so important that it can be wise to attend a "lesser" school to study with a better teacher, rather than to attend a "name" school to study with a teacher who is not a good match. Note that students in majors other than performance are often required to take at least a few semesters of applied study, and are also impacted by the choice of applied teacher.

QUESTIONS RELATED TO APPLIED TEACHERS

Here are a few more questions related to applied teachers. These questions should be asked at some point in the search for schools, preferably before the applicant has spent money on applications and auditions:

- What is the background of each teacher? For example, find out if they are orchestral musicians, soloists, film or studio musicians, composer/arrangers, chamber musicians, or primarily teaching professors. It can be helpful if the teacher's "specialty" mirrors the interests of the student.

- What is the size of the teacher's studio (that is, how many students)?

- Are there multiple teachers of the applicant's instrument? If so, how does the school assign teachers? Is there any crossover between teachers, or are the studios quite discrete?

- Is the teacher well-liked by his or her students? Do the students get along with each other? Do students from different studios get along with each other?

- Does the teacher or the department hold studio classes (in which students play for each other)? If so, how often?

- How often is the teacher on campus? Weekly lessons are the norm. Is the selected teacher available weekly? Does the teacher have an assistant? (Sometimes a student works with an assistant more than with the teacher.) What is the school's policy if the teacher is gone for an extended period?

- Are there any indications that the teacher may be moving to a different school? It is possible for a teacher to take his or her students along when the teacher moves to a different school. However, this can have academic and financial implications for the student.

- What is the "track record" of the teacher's students? Do they win job auditions or competitions? Do they get accepted into highly respected graduate programs? Are they successfully making a living in music?

HELPFUL HINT: FINDING THE NEXT GENERATION

Dorothy DeLay (1917-2002) was a renowned violin teacher at The Juilliard School. Her students included Itzhak Perlman, who has taught at The Juilliard School since 2003. Mr. Perlman's former teaching assistant, Francesca dePasquale, is currently on the faculty of Rutgers University Mason Gross School of the Arts. This is how one finds the next generation of teachers.

THE QUESTION NOT TO ASK

Here is the one question that no one should ask at this point:

- *How much does the school cost?*

This is a big question, but it does not matter yet since financial aid and scholarships have not been offered.

The list of schools should be getting rather long by now. That is okay. The list will be narrowed down, but at this point the applicant needs to see the breadth of choices.

SAFETY, MATCH, AND REACH SCHOOLS

High school counselors define the terms for three types of schools: A *safety* school is one where a particular applicant can easily be admitted.

A *match school* is one where a particular applicant matches the school's profile of admitted students. A *reach school* is one with an exceptionally low admit rate; in other words, the odds are against most applicants being admitted.

For example, Harvard admits less than 6% of it applicants on average; therefore, it is a reach school for almost every student applying. By contrast, Arizona State University is a safety school for most applicants because it admits over 80% of its applicants, on average.

Applicants should remember that regardless of the school's admit rate, the chances of being admitted are different for each applicant. Also, the categories of safety, match, and reach schools are more nuanced for music admissions than for "regular" college admissions.

The most selective music schools (Juilliard, Curtis, Colburn) accept less than 10% of their applicants. But that does not take into account the applied studios. A school can accept 50% of its applicants overall, but if the bassoon studio has one opening and forty applicants then the studio's acceptance rate will be only 2.5%. These numbers may vary from year to year, so it may be worth finding out the acceptance rate by studio, or at least for the music program. Ultimately, an applicant has zero chance of being admitted if they don't apply, and so in that sense the acceptance rate is irrelevant. If an applicant wants to attend a specific school to study with a specific teacher, then they must apply in order to have a chance. Period.

Students who are not majoring in music performance are frequently encouraged to apply to ten to fifteen institutions in order to cover safety, match, and reach schools. Because music performance majors must take into account audition preparation, the cost of audition travel, and the necessary recovery time between the live auditions, they usually apply to fewer schools than general college applicants. With most

43

auditions taking place during a twelve-week window (typically January through March), applying to a smaller number of schools means more time to focus on each audition.

MUSIC MAJOR APPLICATION MATRIX

While teaching at the Colburn School of Performing Arts in Los Angeles and working with high school students planning to major in music, Dr. Annie Bosler designed an algorithm known as the Music Major Application Matrix to help students narrow down the list and give them a strong chance of getting into one of their schools of choice. **This matrix is designed for majors that have an audition requirement.**

The Music Major Application Matrix has proven so effective for Dr. Bosler that she has a 100% success rate using this matrix with her students, who have landed spots in music conservatories all around the United States, Canada, and Europe.

NARROWING THE LIST

After making a broad list of schools, the next step is to narrow it down. That is where the Music Major Application Matrix comes in. The Matrix breaks the list of schools down into four tiers, based on the admit rates *to the studio*. The applicant has to discover these admit rates through research. The key questions to ask are:

(1) What is the typical size of the studio (that is, the number of students studying with a particular teacher)?

(2) How many openings are there this year? If the applicant's private teacher does not know how many openings there will be in a studio, then the applicant should speak with the music admission office or the desired applied teacher.

Note that the Matrix does not use the overall admit rate for the institution, because that may be a very different ratio than the one for an individual studio.

THE TIERS OF THE MUSIC MAJOR APPLICATION MATRIX

Once the two questions above have been answered, it is time to place each school on your list into a tier. Here is how the tiers are divided:

- **Tier One**

  5% or less admit rate (for example, only 0-2 students out of 40 applicants are offered admission to that studio)

- **Tier Two**

  5-10% admit rate (for example, 2-4 students out of 40 applicants are offered admission to that studio)

- **Tier Three**

  10-25% admit rate (for example, 4-10 students out of 40 applicants are offered admission to that studio)

- **Tier Four Schools**

  25-100 % admit rate (for example, 10-40 students out of 40 applicants are offered admission to that studio)

The exercise of breaking down a long list into tiers is all about the school or studio, not about the applicant's ability. For example, a music school may have two clarinet teachers. Clarinet Teacher 1 typically has 10 students in their studio. Clarinet Teacher 2 typically has five students. Both teachers have one student graduating, which means they each have one opening for the coming year. If there are 40 applicants, both of these studios would be Tier 1 studios because they are each accepting only one student with a 5% or less admit rate. If Teacher 1 has three students graduating, then that studio becomes a Tier 2 studio because there is a 7.5% admit rate.

If an applied area has two openings and ten applicants, any applicant has a one-in-five chance of being admitted (20% admit rate), no matter what the applicant's playing level. If an instrument area has two openings and 50 applicants, any applicant has a one-in-25 chance of being admitted (4% admit rate). Note that a particular studio may be in a different tier in different years depending on the number of openings and the number of applicants.

To recap, at this point the applicant has used tools such as networking and online research to develop a fairly long list of schools. Dividing schools into the four tiers helps to sort them and organize the list. This also may help shorten the list by choosing tiers into which the schools fit.

THE APPLICANT'S TIER

The next step is to determine the applicant's tier. This requires the student and their private teacher to make an honest assessment of the student's playing level. Together, the student and teacher should ask these questions: "On an average day at this point, into what tier of schools would the student be accepted? Where does the student's current playing fall?" Determining the student's tier is based on the assumption that the teacher will have knowledge of the schools on the student's college list, an idea of the level of admitted applicants at each school, an understanding of the level of the student's ability on an average day, and also a clear view of the student's audition ability at this point in time, all compared to the average quality of the schools on the student's list. Once the average tier is ascertained, use the following chart to determine the spread across the tiers. This should result in the list being narrowed down to about seven schools.

THE SPREAD

Student Avg. = Tier 1	Student Avg. = Tier 2	Student Avg. = Tier 3	Student Avg. = Tier 4
Tier One Schools = 4	Tier One Schools = 2	Tier One Schools = 1	Tier One Schools = 0
Tier Two Schools = 1	Tier Two Schools = 2	Tier Two Schools = 2	Tier Two Schools = 2
Tier Three Schools = 1	Tier Three Schools = 2	Tier Three Schools = 3	Tier Three Schools = 2
Tier Four Schools = 1	Tier Four Schools = 1	Tier Four Schools = 1	Tier Four Schools = 3
TOTAL = 7	TOTAL = 7	TOTAL = 7	TOTAL = 7

To put this chart into words, if a student is quite advanced, then it is appropriate to aspire to a Tier One school—a school with very competitive admissions. Strategically, however, that student's choice of schools should also include one each of the other tiers, in order to avoid the situation in which they have applied to and been rejected from all Tier One schools. (Recall that the tiers are based on the number of openings in a particular studio at a particular school. With limited openings, even very advanced applicants may be denied admission.)

On the opposite end of the spectrum, if a student is not very advanced, it would be a waste of time, effort, and money to apply to any Tier One

47

school. Therefore, the spread here is two schools from both Tier Two and Tier Three, and three schools from Tier Four.

By honestly assessing where the student's ability falls and then using the spread detailed above, the student will have created a strategic advantage in the college application process. Instead of blindly applying to schools that are either impossible reaches or unchallenging safeties, the applicant now has a list that is researched, targeted, and likely to result in a good outcome.

TRUE STORY

Samantha was a horn student who had taken lessons for only two years. She decided in her senior year that she wanted to major in music performance in college. On an average day, Samantha would get into a Tier Three school. She started with a list of twenty schools, which she then narrowed down to seven using the Music Major Application Matrix.

> **Student Avg. = Tier 3**
> Tier One Schools = 1
> Tier Two Schools = 2
> Tier Three Schools = 3
> Tier Four Schools = 1
> TOTAL = 7

Samantha's top choice was a Tier Two school, possibly considered a reach for her. By using the strategies in this book along with lots of practice, Samantha ended up getting into six of seven schools, including her top choice Tier Two School!

from Annie Bosler

THE SPREAD WITH PRESCREENING RECORDINGS

Many schools require an applicant to submit a recording before being granted an audition; these recordings are referred to as "prescreening recordings" (see Appendix 9 for information on making these recordings). When determining an applicant's tier, the number of schools that require prescreening recordings should be considered.

Applying to seven schools is recommended because it allows the student to apply to schools in and around their average tier. However, applicants have applied to as many as fourteen schools and to as few as one school.

If a student wants to apply to more than seven schools, consider these questions:

- *Calendar:* How many weekends will I be gone to take auditions? How many of those weekends are in a row? How many days of school will need to be missed, and what is my high school's policy on absences? How will I catch up on missed class time and homework?

- *Money:* Add up the number of plane flights, hotels, food, rental cars, application fees, etc. Is this amount worth the extra schools? Is this too much for my bank account?

- *Audition Peaking:* If I apply to ten schools, will I be able to perform my best all ten times?

If a student wants to apply to fewer than seven, take these things into account:

- *Prescreening recordings:* Do I have enough schools that don't require prescreening? Meaning, if I do not get past the prescreen round, do I still have schools where I can audition live?

- *Guarantee (safety) schools:* Do I feel like I have schools on my list that are guaranteed to accept me, even on my worst day?

If 85% or more of the applicant's chosen schools require prescreening recordings, a slightly larger list is desirable, as follows:

Student Avg. = Tier 1	Student Avg. = Tier 2	Student Avg. = Tier 3	Student Avg. = Tier 4
Tier One Schools = 6	Tier One Schools = 3	Tier One Schools = 1	Tier One Schools = 0
Tier Two Schools = 2	Tier Two Schools = 4	Tier Two Schools = 3	Tier Two Schools = 2
Tier Three Schools = 1	Tier Three Schools = 2	Tier Three Schools = 5	Tier Three Schools = 3
Tier Four Schools = 1	Tier Four Schools = 1	Tier Four Schools = 1	Tier Four Schools = 5
TOTAL = 10	TOTAL = 10	TOTAL = 10	TOTAL = 10

Once you receive your prescreening results from all schools, you may choose to withdraw your application from some of those schools prior to the live auditions if you feel your list is too long.

IT'S NOT ALL ABOUT THE SCHOOL'S REPUTATION

With any college search, there can be the temptation to be seduced by the prominence of a school. Deciding to become a music therapist and then wanting to go to Juilliard won't work—Juilliard does not have a music therapy major.

Do your research, and find the school that can teach you how to build the career that you want to have. It might be a small institution that you have never heard of before, but it will end up being a perfect fit.

APPLYING TO MUSIC SCHOOLS OUTSIDE THE U.S.

This topic is a book in itself. Rather than go into detail, here is some food for thought for those U.S. citizens who are considering completing an undergraduate degree abroad.

- Is the student fluent in the language of the country where they want to study?

- Has the student prepared with appropriate study in aural skills and music theory? (Schools outside the U.S. often require a higher level of facility in these areas for incoming students than similar schools in the U.S.)

- Has the student connected with the applied teacher already, through summer study or by visiting the school?

- Perhaps most importantly, the student should have a clear understanding of why they wish to complete their undergraduate education abroad.

To identify schools outside of the U.S., use the same process outlined within this book for gathering and narrowing down schools. Pay very close attention to deadlines as they may differ from U.S. schools.

THE APPLICATION

5

College applications can be daunting for many students (and parents). Schools have different requirements, processes, and even different online application systems. Here is the key point about the application process: *It is an exchange of information.* The stress-reducing strategy here is to *be organized.* This chapter will provide ways to help with this process.

Here are the basic elements of most college applications, music schools or otherwise:

- The actual application form
- The application fee (or fee waiver)
- High school transcript
- Recommendations
- A personal statement or essay
- SAT/ACT scores
- TOEFL (or an equivalent test) for speakers of English as a foreign language

For everyone involved—applicant, parent, school counselor, or teacher— life will be much saner if an application checklist is made and followed. In fact, if the applicant is really organized, this is something that can be started the summer before senior year in high school. Our sample Application Materials Organizer (see Appendix 4) lists a large number of requirements, but not all schools will require all items. For music students in particular, some schools may require prescreening as well, and an audition or interview (depending on the major). If there is a question about any of the required materials, ask the Admissions Office.

THE APPLICATION FORM

By filling out the application form and submitting it, one officially becomes an applicant to the school. The basic purpose of the application form is to provide personal data and demographic information. This information is what will become the applicant's record in a school's database and, if the applicant enrolls, it will morph into the applicant's permanent student record. Without an application on file, the applicant does not exist, and no offer of admission or financial aid can be made.

Sections of the Application Form may include:

- Personal, educational, and demographic data (name, address, contact information, high school information, standardized test scores, etc.)
- Honors and awards
- Extracurricular activities
- Volunteer work
- Portfolio or supplemental application material

Many schools have joined together and decided to use one application form in order to minimize the work for applicants. Here are the main types of application forms and the approximate number of schools that use each:

- Common Application: approximately 700 schools
- Coalition for Access, Affordability, and Success Application: approximately 100 schools

TRUE STORY

An online application was submitted by a student named Rober. I told my assistant that she had mistyped his name, and that it must be Robert. She said that since he had typed his own application, we could only assume that his name was Rober, so that's what we did. We called him Rober during much of the application season, until we learned from his other application materials that his name really was Robert.

My point? If the applicant can't proof his own application (or spell his own name), how am I supposed to know that he is suitable college material?

Moral of the story: This is your college application. Always proofread!

from Kathleen Tesar

THE APPLICATION FEE AND FEE WAIVERS

An application fee is required when submitting an application. Fees can range from $25 to $200 or more. For a typical online application, paying the fee is a step in completing and submitting the application. Never, ever, EVER let the application fee be a barrier to applying. If a student wishes to apply to a school with an application fee of $150 and the student does not have the means to pay that fee, check the application instructions or ask the Admissions Office about a fee waiver. This cannot be stressed enough. Yes, submitting a fee waiver may be an extra step in the process, but for a student who wishes to go to college the effort is worth it.

There are several ways to apply for a fee waiver:

1. The College Board, which administers the SAT, provides SAT test fee waivers and also a limited number of college application fee waivers to qualified students: https://satresourcecenter. collegeboard.org/college-application-fee-waivers.

2. The National Association for College Admission Counseling (NACAC) also provides a limited number of college application fee waivers to qualified students: http://www.nacacnet. org/studentinfo/feewaiver/Pages/default.aspx.

3. The ACT administration provides ACT test fee waivers and a limited number of college application fee waivers to qualified students: http://www.actstudent.org/faq/feewaiver.html

4. In the event a fee waiver form is not available to the applicant, some schools will accept documentation of need, if it is vouched for in writing by someone who knows the applicant's financial situation. For example, a minister or high school counselor may verify that a student is unable to pay the application fee.

5. For Common Application schools, many of these schools accept the request for a fee waiver by the high school counselor who submits the school report for the student. There are criteria by which the high school counselor can verify that a student qualifies (e.g., Title I: Federal lunch program, etc.).

If an applicant is unable to find information for a school's application fee waiver policy online, write directly to the admissions office (see Appendix 5).

HELPFUL HINT:
SAT TEST PREP, SCORES, AND FEE WAIVERS

The SAT is offered at least seven times per year in the United States, and up to six times a year internationally. To schedule an SAT test, visit www.sat.org. There are many different test prep programs, but a common one is Khan Academy Resources. Khan Academy teamed up with College Board, and they now have an SAT "Daily Practice" app where students can access SAT sample questions and practice tests. The app will automatically score the test for you. Visit: www.satpractice. org. Two other great sites are www.sat.org/studygroup and www.youtube.com/collegeboard.

For most schools you send your best overall SAT score from one test date; however, some colleges will use "superscoring" where they take the best scores across multiple test dates.

The SAT also offers a fee waiver to students demonstrating financial need. Those students can receive up to two fee waivers for the SAT registration, four SAT score reports, and four college application fee waivers. Visit: www.collegeboard.org/feewaiver.

TRANSCRIPTS

A transcript is the official document containing the student's academic record, including courses taken, grades earned, and grade point average (GPA). Students must request the transcript from their high school. Students should check with the high school counselor as to whether the school sends the official document to the college or whether the student is responsible for picking it up and sending it. A first-time, first-year applicant (typically meaning a high school senior) will be sending an incomplete transcript when they apply to college because the transcript must be submitted before the student graduates from high school. If an offer of admission is made, it may be "contingent upon successful completion of the applicant's current program." The student will be required to submit a final transcript verifying graduation before starting college. Even if a college has admitted an applicant, the offer may be withdrawn if the final transcript reflects severe slacking-off in the final semesters (also known as "senioritis").

In the case of homeschooling, there is a wide variety of approaches to documenting the applicant's academic record. Homeschooled applicants should check with each admissions office to find out what is considered acceptable documentation of studies.

HELPFUL HINT: WHAT TO DO WHEN A TRANSCRIPT HAS SOME BAD GRADES

Honesty is the best policy. An explanation goes a long way. Kathleen Tesar gives this example:

If I am looking at a record that shows solid grades for two years, and then a serious drop in grades, and a letter from the school counselor or the applicant explains that a family member passed away unexpectedly, then I know that the low grades are not necessarily typical of the applicant. (And sadly, I have read a number of letters like this.) A less traumatic example is when students overextend themselves academically and suffer a drop in GPA for a semester or two. If you cannot find a place to submit this information, send a letter to the admissions office or include the letter when mailing the transcript.

Grades that start strong in the ninth grade and decline raise more concerns than grades that start low and improve. However, the least acceptable explanation is, "I'm a musician, so I don't have to have good grades." That answer will not work at all. It is recommended to consult with your school teacher(s) and counselor(s) to find a tutor to help improve grades in certain classes. It is always better to catch this early than to fall behind in a class or subject area.

RECOMMENDATIONS

Recommendations are meant to round out the applicant's profile. What a school hopes for is insight into the personality of the applicant—their work habits, character, ability for college-level work, etc. What a school usually gets is a generic statement of how wonderful the student is. One of the ways applicants can help recommenders is to let them know why they are applying to the schools, as well as any other information applicants feel will help them write a strong recommendation.

For instance, if a student asks for a recommendation to Cleveland Institute of Music, and is applying for the BM program in composition, the writer can include information about the student's composition skills and experience. If the student is applying to the BM program in piano performance, the recommender can describe how the student has evolved as a pianist, how they work, how often they perform, etc. This information is more helpful to the school than a simple, "He's a good musician." Certainly, if the student is applying to a specific scholarship, the recommender needs to know the criteria so that the letter can be very specific. Remember that it is the student who must supply the information to the recommender. Some teachers or counselors have students fill out a self-assessment form to highlight their accomplishments. It can be helpful for the student to supply their résumé to the recommender. Do not expect or ask the recommenders to do their own research.

Another way to help the recommender is to provide clear instructions on how to submit the recommendation. In the rare instances when a paper recommendation is requested, the protocol is to provide the recommender with an envelope already addressed and with a postage stamp on it. This way the recommender just writes the letter, places it in the envelope, and sends it in the mail.

If the recommendation letter must be written by the recommender and then sent via email, make sure the recommender has the correct email address.

If the school uses recommendation software, make sure the recommender is aware that he or she will be receiving an email with a link to the school's software.

Above all, make sure the recommender knows the deadline. It is the applicant's responsibility to inform the recommender of the deadline. Ideally, the applicant should ask for the recommendation four weeks before the application deadline. Many music conservatories have an application deadline of December 1, which is earlier than many non-music school deadlines. If the recommender has not submitted the recommendation, make sure to remind them of the deadline date. If the applicant has had to create an online application account, they can usually check there to see if recommendations have been received.

ESSAY/PERSONAL STATEMENT

The dreaded essay! Remember, the school wants to know about the applicant. The essay is one more way to give this information. The school may have a specific list of questions from which to choose, or there may be vague instructions to "tell us why you want to come to school here." In any case, the essay should be written by the student. Yes, that's right. Not by the parent, teacher, or paid consultant. Please see Appendix 6 for sample personal statement questions.

Here are some straightforward tips:

- The applicant should read and understand the essay instructions. They are not the same from school to school.

- Once the applicant has written the essay, ask another person to proofread it for typos and grammatical errors. (Note: This is *not* the same as having a parent rewrite the essay.)

- If the applicant is planning ahead, a first draft can be prepared the summer prior to senior year. Many schools update their applications during the summer, so students can look ahead and see the essay questions. By writing a draft during the summer, students can become clear about what they are seeking from an institution; when it comes time to write the actual essay, the process will be less stressful because it was already begun.

- There are some organizations (similar to standardized test tutoring) that will help students organize, develop, and proof personal statements. This is an extra fee, but worthwhile if the student has many essays to write. (Note that an applicant getting help to develop an essay is not the same as paying someone to write the essay for the applicant. Most admissions officers can detect an essay that has been written by someone else, and it is considered dishonest.)

HELPFUL HINT: AVOID THIS ESSAY MISTAKE

Admissions officers understand that students are applying to more than one school. They also understand that students prefer not to write six different essays when one can be reused. But DO NOT forget to change the school's name in the essay!

On more than one occasion Kathleen Tesar has received essays that began with, "I want to study at the New England Conservatory because..." The only problem was that they were submitted to the Colburn School.

SUPPLEMENTAL FORMS AND MATERIALS

Supplemental forms and materials may be required in addition to the application form to give more specific information to the schools. Not every degree or major will require supplemental items, but if they do, the purpose is to obtain further information about the applicant. For example, a composition applicant will have to provide scores; a music history major may have to send in a sample research paper. In some cases, supplemental materials will be optional, but providing materials may strengthen the application.

Here is a list of additional items that a school may request:

- A recording (either prescreening or supplemental)

- A résumé (see Appendix 7)

- A repertoire list (see Appendix 8)

- A supplemental application for a specific major

- Scores (especially for majors in composition or arranging)

- Portfolio of work for a specific major (e.g., recording engineering, conducting, etc.)

In certain situations, *supplemental* recordings (not *prescreening* recordings) may be required from students wishing to major in an area of music other than performance, or to minor in music. Supplemental recordings are also very useful for non-music majors who want to present a well-rounded application. Supplemental recordings, as implied by the name, are NOT crucial to the admission process. Each school is different and has different requirements for recordings (in repertoire, number of minutes, format, etc.), so make sure to thoroughly check the school's website for details. For those wishing to make a supplemental recording, see Appendix 9 and use the same guidelines as outlined for a prescreening tape.

TRUE STORY

One of my private horn students applying to Stanford University for a business major decided to submit a supplemental recording along with his application. He spent time practicing and recording the two contrasting pieces required. Once he was accepted to the school, he had a chat with one of the admissions officers at Stanford in regards to his acceptance. The officer said that they receive a lot of applications with similar qualifications (GPA, SAT, etc.); however, the student's dedication to music along with his supplemental recording set him apart from the other applicants. The student decided to go to Stanford and even played in the Stanford Symphony Orchestra.

from Annie Bosler

Do not send in supplemental materials that are NOT requested. To illustrate this point, the University of Pennsylvania specifically *discourages* sending supplemental materials:

> Most students who are admitted to Penn do not submit supplemental materials. All of the information that we feel is crucial in making an admissions decision is contained within our required documents. There are some students for whom some additional information can be beneficial, but we recommend that you think very carefully before sending in supplementary material. If information is already included somewhere in your application, that information does not need to be submitted again in supplemental form. In most cases, too many extra documents can take away from the strength of an application:

https://admissions.upenn.edu/admissions-and-financial-aid/
what-penn-looks-for/supplementary-materials.

HELPFUL HINT: SENDING APPLICATION MATERIALS

Never send required application materials to faculty members. Always send them to the Admissions Office, so that the
staff can note that you submitted them. Then it is the staff's
job to make sure the faculty members see the materials.

PRESCREENING RECORDINGS:
A SPECIAL KIND OF SUPPLEMENTAL MATERIAL

Music schools that have large applicant pools use prescreening recordings to narrow down the top candidates. In effect, prescreening creates
an additional round to the audition process. The applicant is required to
record and submit some or all of the audition repertoire to determine if
they can proceed to the next step in the audition process. At this point, an
applicant may be denied admission and not invited to proceed further.
Be aware that it takes time for the faculty to review these prescreening
recordings. It is wise to wait until notification that the student has successfully passed the prescreening round before making any travel plans.

HELPFUL HINTS: RECORDING YOURSELF

Appendix 9 has great details about making a prescreening
recording, but here are a few hints:

- Making a recording is an involved process, and it always
  takes more time than planned. Be sure to build plenty of

time into your schedule. You do not want to be frazzled or submit something that does not reflect your true ability.

- If the requirement is to perform the music from memory, do not put the music stand off-camera and then pretend you have it memorized.

- If you are a pianist, do not audition on an upright piano.

- Always have a third party (usually your teacher) review the recording before you submit it. ALWAYS. If the sound quality is poor, don't send it in. Redo it.

- Never assume that "it's just prescreening." This recording must be taken as seriously as the audition itself. It IS an audition!

PORTFOLIOS

For those students who know before they apply that they want to major in an area of music outside of performance, check for any "portfolio" requirements. A portfolio is a collection of works or documents that are representative of a person's skills and accomplishments. The items in a portfolio should be examples of the student's most impressive work. The portfolio should be put together carefully and not thrown together at the last minute. Just as an art applicant would submit a portfolio of art that they created in the years prior to college applications, a student wishing to major in an area of music other than performance should begin putting together a portfolio for that area at least a year ahead of time. For example, if planning to major in music recording, the portfolio requirements often include several examples of recordings the student has made and edited.

DIG DEEPER: PORTFOLIOS

To better understand the idea of portfolios, here are a couple of links:

- CalArts: https://calarts.edu/admissions/portfolio-audition/music/music-technology
- NACAC Performing Arts College Fairs: http://www.nacac-net.org/college-fairs/pva-college-fairs/pages/default.aspx

TRANSFER APPLICANTS

In this book we are assuming (for the most part) that the college applicant is a high school senior. However, there are many paths to music study, and not all of them follow this course. In general, transferring between schools is fairly common. Here is some information on how that works.

First, the definition of a transfer applicant: If a student has finished high school and has taken classes at a post-secondary institution, they are considered a transfer applicant. Period. *(Note: This definition does not pertain to high school students who took college classes before graduating from high school.)* The transfer applicant does not get to decide that "I want to apply as a freshman," or "I want to enter as a junior." This is because of the basic rule of transferring from one post-secondary institution to another: the new school makes that determination.

Each school has its requirements for degrees and majors. The school defines how many units of each requirement a student must complete in order to graduate with a specific degree and major. The situation is even more specific in music schools, where so much of what is taught is skill-based. Music theory, aural skills, and keyboard skills are requirements for most music degrees, and each school determines the number of credits required to graduate. No matter how many credits a student has earned at one school, the new school will not accept those credits without validating competency by administering an exam. This can be an advantage, however, because students with advanced skills can receive credit by exam and thus lighten their course load somewhat—even as freshmen.

HELPFUL HINT: PLACEMENT EXAMS

One way for music students to get ahead on college courses is to study music theory and piano in high school, and to develop aural skills alongside theory and piano. When it comes time to take placement exams for college courses, students who have a grounding in these areas can earn credit. And, in these situations, credit earned is time saved, which means more time to spend in the practice room!

Part of the transfer situation is something called "articulation agreements." These are formal agreements between institutions that spell out which credits earned at one school will be accepted at the other. If a student wishes to graduate from a four-year institution and begins at a two-year community college, it is indeed possible to save time and money by completing core general education requirements at the community college and transferring those credits to a university that has an articulation agreement with the community college. However, most conservatories have very different core requirements and also place students based on skills. If the student doesn't develop their musical skills (in theory, ear training, keyboard harmony, etc.) while in community college, then it may take more than four years to earn an undergraduate degree.

Here is a good explanation of articulation agreements, with links to a database of agreements: http://www.collegetransfer.net/AskCT/Whatisan Articulation Agreement/tabid/3417/Default.aspx.

SUMMARY

When the student is drowning in application paperwork, it is helpful to remember that each school requires different application materials because each school IS different. The applicant's job is to provide all the required information by the deadline, and then to focus on the audition day. Refer to Appendix 4 for the Application Materials Organizer. It will help.

Students, remember: If you have not submitted the application, you are not an applicant. Schools can only offer admission and financial aid to applicants. If you do not apply, you are not an applicant and therefore you will not be admitted and will not be offered any money.

Also remember this: The quality of your application and application materials is a reflection of yourself. Missing information, misspelled words, and incomplete materials all shine a negative light on you. At the extreme, an applicant who submits false information (such as a plagiarized essay or an altered transcript) may be dismissed from consideration. When you submit all the application requirements on time and in good order, that speaks positively about your seriousness of purpose. Be one of those applicants.

ORGANIZING AND PRACTICING FOR PERFORMANCE AUDITIONS

6

A good strategy for any student is to make a chart organizing all the components of college applications. Music performance majors have the additional challenge of the audition—finding the lists of required audition repertoire, practicing efficiently, making arrangements to attend auditions, keeping up with schoolwork, and remaining physically and mentally healthy throughout the whole process. Majors other than performance may still require an audition, or the submission of other materials. Being organized is the best way for any applicant in any major to reduce the inevitable stress of applying to college. More organizational tools can be found in the Appendices.

ORGANIZING THE REPERTOIRE LISTS

Music schools and departments create lists of specific audition requirements in order to assess applicants consistently. For performance majors, there will be a list of required repertoire that may include solo estral excerpts, études, scales, arpeggios, and sight-reading. ols are very specific in their requirements for the audition, while others are very general. (For example, see Appendix 10 and compare the trombone list at the Colburn School to the list at California State University, Long Beach.)

The best recommendation for applicants is to use a three-ring binder to organize all of the repertoire lists, music, charts, and master lists. This binder will be referred to as the Repertoire Binder.

Step 1: Make an audition information spreadsheet

The audition information spreadsheet (see Appendix 11) is a simple tool that can be used to manage all of the prescreening deadlines and audition dates. Once completed, place this as the first page of the Repertoire Binder as a goal-setting reminder. This spreadsheet should be shared with the private teacher to help prepare for a peak performance at each audition.

Step 2: Gather the audition repertoire list for each school

As early as sophomore or junior year of high school, a student can start to look at audition repertoire lists. Even if the student is not yet ready to tackle the repertoire, it is good to know what they will have to prepare.

A student might be required to learn a large amount of music for the audition—possibly as much as twenty minutes to an hour of music— even though the committee will not listen to all of it. Students who begin learning some of this repertoire early in their high school career can put it away for a while, and then come back to it before the actual auditions. This gives a student the advantage of having a few years of familiarity with the repertoire. Remember that decisions about repertoire and preparation should always be discussed with the private teacher.

To find the repertoire lists:

1. Go to the school's website.

2. Look under "Admissions" or "Prospective Students," "Audition Information," and then the specific instrument or vocal specialty. (Different schools may organize the information differently, but this is generally how to find it.) Make sure to choose the list of audition requirements for the correct degree program. (Lists for graduate programs are typically lengthier, with more difficult repertoire.)

3. Print a copy of each school's audition list and add it to the Repertoire Binder.

Repertoire lists generally are finalized by September 1, which is when most music school applications go live. If the student has researched the list prior to September 1, make sure to check again at the beginning of the academic year in which the student is applying, in case there are any changes.

See Appendix 10 for an example of audition repertoire lists by school.

Step 3: Make a master repertoire list

No later than the beginning of senior year in high school, take all the repertoire lists and combine them into one list. For this list, do not worry about which school requires which piece. This list is a way of seeing all the music an applicant has to prepare for auditions at his or her chosen schools, rather than having to refer to multiple lists (see Appendix 12).

Some schools require one list of repertoire for the prescreening rounds and a different list for the live audition rounds. Other schools will add to the prescreening list for the live auditions. Therefore, on this master list, indicate if the repertoire is for the prescreening round, the live audition round, or both. Since prescreening recordings are due December 1 for most conservatories, many students start working on prescreening repertoire in the summer between junior and senior years. If live audition repertoire is different than prescreening repertoire, it is still highly recommended that applicants prepare both lists during the summer prior to their senior year in high school.

HELPFUL HINT: HOW TO USE REPERTOIRE LISTS TO YOUR ADVANTAGE

Some institutions have very vague audition requirements—for example, "prepare scales and two contrasting solos." In such cases, use this to your advantage. For schools with unspecified repertoire lists, choose works from your master list that you are learning for another school, and with which you are very comfortable. This strategy helps control the amount of repertoire you have to learn, and gives you multiple opportunities to perform the same repertoire.

Step 4: Organize the Repertoire Binder

Placing all of the music in the Repertoire Binder keeps it together in one place and makes practicing more efficient. Make three tabs within the binder:

- Tab 1: Music for the upcoming audition *(The content in this tab will change as the student completes an audition.)*

- Tab 2: All remaining music for the rest of the auditions

- Tab 3: All the lists of audition repertoire for the individual schools from Step 2.

  Note: Either in the front pocket of the binder or in a sleeve at the front of the binder, keep the audition information spreadsheet from Step 1 and the master repertoire list from Step 3.

Some students wish to create their Repertoire Binder on a tablet (such as an iPad) and use an app to write directly on the music. This works. However, be sure to travel with a power cord, and have the device fully charged for the audition. Also ensure that the sound is off and that screen brightness will remain consistent throughout the audition. For auditions where the applicant is required to bring copies of their music for the audition committee, please take into account that many faculty members still prefer hard copies of the music over digital displays.

TRUE STORY

Paul was auditioning at seven schools. He showed up at School A with a stack of music. Unfortunately, the stack was a mixture of music from several different schools; it was missing some of the pieces required by School A. Thankfully, one of the other applicants let Paul borrow her music. However, the challenge of reading off of someone else's music added to his stress and had a negative impact on how he played. I have heard similar stories from other teachers. Repertoire Binders have been a big hit among all of my students, and the good news is that no one has repeated Paul's story.

from Annie Bosler

PIANO ACCOMPANIMENT

Some schools will require the applicant to have piano accompaniment either for the prescreening recording, for the live audition, or both. Applicants whose audition pieces have piano accompaniment should perform those works as often as possible with a pianist. This gives the student more in-depth knowledge of the music. Familiarity with the piano part is helpful for playing without the accompaniment, and it is critical when performing a piece with a new accompanist at a new school with little or no practice together. Students should also become comfortable playing with pianos tuned at either A440 or A442, since one cannot know a particular piano's tuning ahead of time, and playing in tune with the piano is crucial.

PRACTICING FOR THE AUDITIONS

Practicing for college auditions is a different kind of practicing. There is a defined timeline for learning the music, very specific repertoire requirements, and a definite outcome. The level of commitment must be more intense, and the work must be much more detailed. The following five steps offer a way of practicing that addresses these needs.

Step 1: Listening

This type of practicing does not involve singing or playing the instrument. Make a playlist of the audition repertoire and listen to it frequently while following along reading the music. If listening to an aria, concerto, or an orchestral excerpt, try following the full score, in addition to following the featured part. This kind of preparation, without singing or playing, actually saves time and improves the efficiency of learning the material when practicing. While listening, make marks or brackets around the spots that may seem tricky and will need slow repetition.

Step 2: Woodshedding

In this second phase, practice is very slow and methodical. The term "woodshedding" or "shedding" refers to chipping away at the challenges and difficulties of a piece (out in the "woodshed" or somewhere isolated away from other people). It is heavy technical work. A metronome is used all the time. Notes, rhythms, articulations and bowings, sound quality, style, and intonation are all given close attention. No detail is too small to be examined. Musicians return to this step to work out difficult technical passages, but as audition preparation moves forward they spend less and less time woodshedding passages. A good place to start woodshedding is with the spots marked or bracketed from Step 1.

Step 3: Polishing

The goal now is to make the selection sound natural and organic. It is less about technical work (which was completed in Step 2), and more about being able to play or sing large sections of the music fluidly and consistently. The focus should be on style, expression, musicality, and "selling" the passage or piece to the listener.

Step 4: Performing

In an actual audition, the applicant must be able to play or sing straight through a work with complete focus. Auditioners must be able to switch from concerto to excerpt to scale to etude, performing each convincingly. Start by setting the goal of playing or singing through a work in the practice room, beginning to end, no matter what happens. Then, set up mock auditions (mock audition options are outlined in Chapter 7) and perform the work for friends, family, and/or teachers. Set the same goal: play or sing through from start to finish, no matter what. If there is a lot of solo repertoire, schedule several performances at local nursing homes, children's hospitals, churches, etc. The applicant that will stand out in the audition is the one that sounds prepared, confident, convincing, and has something to express musically.

Step 5: Tapering

An often overlooked process, especially with a number of auditions happening very close to each other in time, is the concept of tapering. Although most students want to spend more time physically practicing, it is important to decrease practice time two to three days prior to the real audition. This is counterintuitive—the usual urge is to practice even more the day or two before the actual audition. By following Steps 1-4 above, the applicant will benefit from reducing the physical demands of intense practice in the last few days before the audition. The idea is to go into the audition fresh and rested. Mental performance (presented in Chapter 7)—different from mental practice outlined below—is very useful during this phase since it requires a minimal expenditure of energy.

MENTAL PRACTICE

Mental practice is silent practice without the instrument or voice. The goal is to recreate a practice session in your imagination, before executing it. Visualize it, feel it, hear it.

Some people refer to this technique as "visualization" or "mental rehearsal." The techniques are similar and all can be developed over time with daily practice. Musicians should try at least 20 minutes per day (in two 10-minute blocks) for one week to see some dramatic improvements. Since mental practice will require repetitions, this goes well with *Step 2: Woodshedding* and *Step 3: Polishing.*

TRUE STORY

I use the technique of mental practice with all of my clients, including professional musicians and Olympic athletes. It has proven to be a very successful tool for winning auditions and gold medals.

I once worked with a very talented high school musician who felt that he never had enough time to prepare pieces, even though he practiced a lot. He was able to perform in front of large audiences, but he never felt prepared for big events, and so he felt guilty. This musician was not using his practice time effectively.

He tried visualizing the phrases in his pieces, hearing them clearly, and feeling his body execute the correct movements before he tried to perform them. He began to realize that if he combined physical practice with mental practice, he accelerated his learning process and was much more efficient. By the time of his next big event, he felt more confident and prepared than ever. He went on to win first prizes in major competitions and was invited to solo with several orchestras.

from Don Greene

MENTAL PRACTICE INSTRUCTIONS FOR THE PERFORMER

Step 1: Identify the passage
Identify a challenging passage in one of your pieces. If you have it memorized, close your eyes. If not, look at the music.

Step 2: Slow mental practice
Sing or play through the passage slowly in your head. This tempo should

be slow enough that you can perform it flawlessly, including playing all the right notes, rhythms, articulations, expression, phrasing, etc.

Step 3: Repeat the passage

If you stumble as you imagine the passage, repeat it even more slowly, until you can execute it flawlessly in your mind. You can use a metronome while you do this.

Step 4: Make the phrase longer

Once the passage is mastered at the desired tempo, go back and weave it into the context of the piece. In other words, start a few measures before the passage and continue mentally playing after it, all flawlessly.

Step 5: Add Centering to mental practice

Once you learn Centering, presented in the following chapter, you can start your mental practice sessions with it.

MENTAL PRACTICE EXAMPLE

You have had a few lessons on a new piece with your teacher, and you are in the process of woodshedding it. Sit down with the music and perform through a passage in your head. Follow the notes on the page, hearing the sound in your inner ear. Feel your instrument or vocal cords in your mind. If you feel yourself stumble in your head, that is where you will stumble with your instrument or voice. Mentally practice the part where you stumbled. Slow the passage down, repeating it many times. Is there a certain note, rhythm, or grouping of notes that is throwing you? If so, break this down further, practicing even more slowly and targeting smaller sections. Using a metronome during mental practice also can be a useful tool. This is an enormously efficient way to practice. It also has the advantage of being something you can do anywhere, anytime. It is not necessary to have the music in front of you, but the visual reference is often helpful.

When students make a habit of incorporating mental practice into their daily routine, then working through tricky, difficult passages takes less time. This skill is not only useful for college auditions but also gives an advantage when learning any scales, études, solos, or memorizing music. Organizing the repertoire and incorporating the five stages of practicing for auditions (listening, woodshedding, polishing, performing, and tapering) will lead to feeling prepared and confident, which in turn will lead inevitably to successful auditions.

TOOLS FOR SUCCESSFUL AUDITIONS

7

Students may encounter many variables while on the college audition circuit: jet lag, differences in weather and altitude, nerves, exhaustion, uncomfortable audition venues with new and unexpected acoustics, to name a few. Through all of this, the student who has prepared for as many of these variables as possible will feel confident about the audition. The professors listening will be swayed by the students who play the most convincing auditions. In this chapter, we introduce the Centering Process, mock auditions, and mental performance.These strategies have proven very successful with high school students, as well as with musicians on the professional audition circuit.

MANAGING NERVES

Managing nerves through the audition process is a topic that is not often addressed in high school. It is important to know some of the causes of nerves: encountering threatening environments, unknown situations, dangerous conditions, or feeling unprepared. The nerves discussed here are specifically related to the performance stress of college auditions, but some of the suggestions can be applied to other performance situations like recitals and juries. Musicians need to learn how performance stress affects them so they can learn how to cope with it successfully.

Performance stress can manifest itself in three different areas: physical symptoms, mental effects, and emotional consequences. Although these symptoms and effects are normal, they often are unhelpful for musicians (for example, when nerves result in the loss of fine motor coordination or poor concentration). Performers may feel that what comes out at the audition is not even close to how they sound in the practice room. Centering is the first step to tackling performance stress.

THE CENTERING PROCESS

The Centering process is a powerful strategy used to counter the symptoms and effects of performance stress. Centering comes from the Japanese martial art Aikido and modern day sports psychology. It works for a number of reasons:

- It gives conscious control of breathing. This is very important, because people who are under pressure tend to breathe shallowly and reduce their oxygen intake, which affects them both physically and mentally.

- It releases tension from muscles. Control over large and small muscles is necessary for accuracy.

- Centering helps performers to switch from their analytical, noisy left brains to their artistic and performance-oriented right brains immediately before they play or sing. Performing in the right brain allows musicians to clearly hear the music, rather than hearing the left brain's critical words and useless chatter.

Parents and teachers are encouraged to learn the Centering process along with their student musicians. It will help teachers and parents to guide students in acquiring and refining this important strategy. As a bonus, the parents and teachers may gain a helpful skill for dealing with their own stress through the next several months.

TRUE STORY

I worked with a musician who had a long history of struggling with auditions. In spite of a Master of Music degree and an extended fellowship at the New World Symphony, he had not won any auditions in four years. His nerves caused problems including erratic tempo choices, over-thinking, and inability to focus.

I first taught him Centering, helping him to switch from his noisy left brain to his quiet, focused right brain. After he used Centering in his practice and mock auditions, his tempo choices became steadier. The better he played, the more his confidence grew. It was not long before he won his first professional audition with the Atlanta Symphony, and after that a principal position with the Cleveland Orchestra.

from Don Greene

CENTERING INSTRUCTIONS

Start by finding a comfortable and balanced position, either sitting or standing. Make sure your back is straight and your feet are placed solidly on the floor. If you are standing, your feet should be shoulder width apart with a slight bend in your knees. Place your hands over your center, two inches below your navel. Visualize the space two inches inwards towards your spine. Make sure you feel that your weight is equally distributed, front to back and side to side.

Step 1: Form your clear intention

Start by forming a clear idea of what you intend to do after you are Centered. State this goal to yourself in precise terms, such as, "I am going to play with confidence and courage." or "I am going to nail the first phrase." For practice at the beginning, the intention can be, "I am going to learn how to Center."

Step 2: Pick your focal point

Direct your eyes to a specific point one to seven feet in front of you. Make sure that this focus point is lower than eye level. This is important because when your eyes go up, you shift into left brain. You are learning how to access the right brain by lowering your gaze. After focusing on your point, close your eyes.

Step 3: Concentrate on your breathing

Inhale slowly through your nose, pause, then exhale slowly through your mouth. Make sure to draw each breath into your abdomen, as low and as deeply as possible. Focus on your breathing for five or more breaths, until you are concentrating only on your breathing.

Step 4: Scan for muscle tension

Inhale slowly through your nose, then pause to see if your jaw feels tight. Feel free to move your jaw around and exhale any tension you find. Next, inhale and pause to check if your neck feels tight. Release any neck tension you find when you exhale. Check your shoulders, pause, and let go of any shoulder tightness while breathing out. Follow the same pattern, monitoring and releasing any tension you find anywhere in your body. (Make sure to check your back and legs for tension, too. Although you may play your instrument primarily with your lips or your hands, you still need to have a solid, reliable base on which to sit or stand.)

Step 5: Be at your center

Breathe deeply into your center. Feel your body from the inside. Get out of your head and into your center. Sense that quiet, solid base. Inhale, feel your center, then exhale. Inhale, be at your center, then breathe out.

Step 6: Imagine it vividly

Briefly imagine performing an excerpt just the way you would like it to go. When you hear the passage clearly, you know that you are in your right brain.

Step 7: Direct your energy

Open your eyes and guide your attention back to your focus point. You are now Centered and ready to begin your performance.

Your ability to Center will improve rapidly with practice. For the next few days, it is recommended that you practice Centering five to seven times per day. If you use it as part of your daily routine, before you warm up, practice, take a lesson, etc., you will soon notice positive effects in your ability to cope successfully with all kinds of stress, especially the high stress of auditions and important concerts. After you practice the seven steps for a week, you will be able to get Centered on demand, before or during any audition or performance.

MOCK AUDITIONS

A mock audition is the perfect place to begin incorporating Centering. The purpose of the mock audition is to create as closely as possible the circumstances of a real audition. The goal is to perform the repertoire list many times, and then to vary the conditions under which it is played, thus learning how the performer reacts under pressure.

Try to set up at least five mock auditions per live audition. This means the applicant should play the list from each specific school five times, in front of an audience, before the actual audition. If the applicant is auditioning at seven schools, then the goal will be to perform 35 mock auditions. However, if it is not possible to get all of the mock auditions in prior to the school's audition, do not feel discouraged. Any number of mock auditions is better than none.

Between junior and senior year, as many students begin to increase practice time on their instrument, it is common to see a high level of musical progress. It is very important for each student to not only to practice the repertoire, but also to practice the act of auditioning in a mock environment with many variables. Students who take advantage of mock auditions will find that live auditions are much less intimidating.

EIGHT AUDITION VARIABLES

Keep this list in mind when scheduling each mock audition.

1. **Rooms:** Auditions take place in many different kinds of rooms. At some schools, the audition may be in a teacher's small studio. At other schools, the audition may be in a 250-seat recital hall. A satellite audition may take place in a gymnasium. The applicant must be prepared to perform in any environment.

2. **Acoustics:** No matter what the size of the room, the applicant has to deal with whether the room is "live" or "dead." A very live room practically echoes, while a very dead room may make it seem like one's tone has no vibrancy at all. Practice not letting the sound that is heard affect the performance—to perform normally in spite of the acoustics.

3. **Temperature and altitude:** How does a cold room affect one's voice or playing? How does a hot room affect it? The audition

may take place at high altitude. Mock auditions can be used to practice playing with as many of these conditions as possible. Practice dealing with sweaty hands, a dry mouth, or cold fingers. Learn how high humidity affects bow hair, how high altitude affects reeds and breath support, etc.

4. **Audiences:** An audition committee may be made up of one person, or five people, or even ten or twelve people. An applicant may be acquainted with some or all of the people listening. So for mock auditions, it is recommended to gather different groups of people to listen to the applicant play the audition repertoire list. The applicant can invite family members, teachers, band/choir/orchestra directors, and friends who sing or play different instruments. Practice performing in front of varying numbers of people.

5. **Distractions:** The audition committee may not be fully focused on the applicant, or at least it can seem that way sometimes. Ask the mock audition audience members to move around, shuffle papers, etc. What if the audition committee eats lunch during the audition? What if someone's phone rings? It is very typical for committee members to take notes. None of these things should affect how the applicant plays, because the applicant will have practiced mock auditions that include distractions.

6. **Repertoire:** The applicant will not know what the committee will ask to hear first, or whether they will hear entire works. The applicant should learn the entire repertoire list as specified by the school, but understand that only part of the list or part of a piece may be performed. Practice the audition repertoire in different orders and with stops in different places. (A great way to do this is to make flash cards that contain the name of each piece, scale, or excerpt. An audience member can pull a card to determine the order.) Often, the committee will give the applicant the option to

choose the first work to perform. Therefore, the applicant should always know with which piece they would like to start if given the choice. Also be prepared to start with scales. Many committees ask for scales as a "warm-up" in the space; however, know all major and all forms of minor scales just in case they are asked.

7. **Transitions:** In the context of auditions, a "transition" is the moment between one piece and the next. Since the applicant will not always know the order of the repertoire, this transition is very important. Most students do not pay attention or plan for this moment; however, this moment can feel like an eternity. What the applicant chooses to do in this moment is crucial to the success of the audition. What professionals have learned to do is create a mental image of each piece that captures a clear feel for the tempo, the style of the piece, and the opening bars in both the solo part and in the accompaniment (if the work is accompanied). Then they use skills such as Centering and a mental image of each work to shift smoothly between pieces.

For example, if the applicant starts with a work by Mozart, and the committee stops the applicant after the opening and asks the applicant to play something by Strauss followed by the prepared étude, how does the applicant mentally make the change? By practicing Centering and seeing the mental image over and over during mock auditions, the transitions will become automatic and feel completely natural, no matter in what order the repertoire is played. Another byproduct of using a mental image of a piece is that it allows the applicant to present a bigger color palette as they move from piece to piece, and demonstrate the differences in genres, styles, and dynamics (i.e., Mozart will sound different than Beethoven which is different from Wagner). This ability to make each piece sound different is a sign that the applicant has a musical understanding that goes beyond the notes, and therefore is a more desirable candidate than one whose pieces all sound the same.

8. **Silence:** A circumstance related to transitions is silence. The committee may not speak to the applicant between pieces, but this should not be a distraction. It is tempting to assume that silence is negative, or that it implies the applicant has to rush through the process. If the applicant has practiced transitioning and followed the routine, the silence will feel like a natural part of the audition. Embrace any silence. Each committee will treat the time or silence between pieces differently. This should not distract the performer.

TRANSITIONS AND PRE-SHOT ROUTINES

In sports, a pre-shot routine is a type of mental strategy used just before a shot is taken. The pre-shot routine is a combination of a mental image, physical feeling, and emotional confidence. For example, a tennis player may imagine where the serve will go, recall the feeling of a relaxed service motion, and feel the confidence from the thousands of serves that have been hit.

As a musician, you can use this same technique of a pre-shot routine to help you transition between pieces. Start to develop your transition routine during practice sessions. Physically feel the tempo and recall the energy of the piece. Then build a mental sound image of your opening notes. Finally, emotionally commit to performing the piece the way you have practiced it over and over. Above all, breathe.

Use your mock auditions to build and practice your mental transition routine.

SET A SIMPLE PERFORMANCE GOAL

Many students set technical and musical goals for an audition. These goals are what the student focuses on in the practice room and works on in lessons. As the student takes auditions, certain performance patterns may become apparent. For example, the rhythm may be steady in the practice room, but at an audition it becomes very unsteady, or the student may find that they use a much smaller dynamic range in an audition.

A simple performance goal can be chosen by focusing on one of these patterns that needs fixing or strengthening. By defining this simple performance goal and coming back to it over and over again in the series of five mock auditions, the student's audition skills will improve.

The next step is to reduce the goal to a very basic concept, a word or phrase the student can use as a mental cue. For example, a singer or brass player could use the word "air" as a reminder to take a nice inhale and send the air to the back of the hall, striving for a full sound. A string player could use "even bow speed" as a reminder not to press. This simple performance goal or cue is then available to the student as a point of focus in auditions.

MOCK AUDITION STRATEGIES

Strategies for organizing an effective mock audition series include the following:

Strategy 1: Choose the audience

- People who know the repertoire and can comment on its performance (i.e., private teacher, vocal coach, orchestra director, friend from band or orchestra, etc.)

- Family

- Friends

- Anyone who makes the student nervous

Note: If a student can't find someone to listen, record the audition on someone's voicemail, or make a recording and send it to someone from the above list.

Strategy 2: Decide what role the audience will have. Choose from these three options:

- Audience listens; player pauses between pieces for comments

- Audience listens; player does not stop; comments are given at the end of the audition

- Audience listens; player does not stop; no comments *(This is the preferred option a few days out from the audition.)*

Strategy 3: Vary repertoire order

Because an applicant cannot anticipate the order in which audition repertoire will be played, it is important to practice mixing up the list. One way to do this is to use the flash card method mentioned earlier in this chapter, so that the order is chosen at random by drawing cards. The student also should have an ideal order for each rep list. This way the student is prepared for a random order of performance, as well as prepared if the committee asks the student to choose the order. Attempt to have one of the mock auditions run in the student's preferred order of pieces, as well as one run with random combinations of repertoire.

Strategy 4: Use adversity training

Adversity training is adding distractions to the mock auditions. Ask the audience to eat, cough, sneeze, shuffle papers, drop something, hum the same excerpt in a different key, or have a cell phone ring while the student is playing. This prepares a student for most of the odd things that might happen during an audition. In adverse mock auditions, the student can figure out the best coping strategies. This is much better than trying to cope for the first time at the real audition.

TRUE STORY

A professional violinist experienced an audition where the performance space and the warm-up room were very close to each other. While the violinist began to play her audition, she could hear the next person warming up on the same repertoire that she was performing! Unfortunately, this was not a distraction for which she had prepared in her practice and the audition did not go as well as she hoped.

from Annie Bosler

Strategy 5: Use simulation training

High-energy practice, known as simulation training, is the optimal way to learn to deal with audition adrenalin. Adrenalin is the body's natural reaction to a stressful situation; it urges a person to fight or run away. This strategy can be practiced in two ways: Students can invite audience members who make them nervous, or they can increase their heart rates by doing jumping jacks, wall squats, or running in place. In either case, the student is creating the physical symptoms that may arise during an audition and practicing how to use the resulting energy.

Strategy 6: Record yourself

Recording and listening to mock auditions and practice sessions can be challenging and time-consuming at first, but recording is a great tool for improvement. Sometimes what the student thinks is coming across to the listener (i.e., rhythm, style, expression, dynamic contrast, etc.) is not. Listening objectively to a recording allows the student to step back from the emotion and stress of striving for excellence, and to take on the role of teacher and committee member—assessing and improving the performance. Recording can also show the student that certain aspects of their performance are going better than they thought.

Strategy 7: Use four steps to quickly recover from mistakes

If the student makes a mistake during the audition, it is best to accept that the mistake happened and mentally leave it behind. The student does not need to be okay with what happened; they just need to get past it. This is part of what is practiced in the mock auditions.

> Step 1: Accept the mistake. Rather than focusing on what may have caused the mistake, the student should bring their mind back to the present, to the note or phrase that needs to be played now. There will be plenty of time to analyze what happened after the student is done playing or singing. Let the mistake go; come back to the present moment.

> Step 2: Relax key muscles. Musicians tend to cringe or tighten up in certain areas after they make a mistake. Before making a second mistake because of muscle tension, the student should make sure to relax the muscles involved in playing well. Use an exhale to drop all tension in those muscles.

> Step 3: Mentally cue the simple performance goal. Have the simple performance goal in mind before beginning any

performance. Re-cue this goal as needed throughout the performance.

Step 4: Stick with the transition plan and routine using Centering and a mental image of the next piece. This will also help with keeping focus in the present moment of the audition.

MOCK AUDITION OUTCOMES

By the time a student has finished a series of mock auditions, the following will have been accomplished:

- The student will be able to play or sing through the audition repertoire list without stopping, using the transition plan and routine that they practiced, no matter what the order of the repertoire.

- The student will have defined the "approach" of the audition so that it can be recreated no matter what the circumstances or repertoire order. By defining the style of each composer and each work so that it is clear they understand the music on a much broader level than accurate notes and rhythms, Mozart will not come out sounding like Stravinsky. Committees enjoy hearing an applicant demonstrate musical maturity.

- The student will know how to navigate any of the eight audition variables.

MENTAL PERFORMANCE

Mental *practice* (presented in Chapter 6) is a way of woodshedding and working through the mechanics of learning a piece. In mental *performance*, the student is mentally living the actual performance. All the details of the performance are there: what outfit is worn, the feeling of walking on the stage, and the sound of one's voice or instrument. The goal is to experience the ideal performance in the mind first, from beginning to end without stopping, before executing it on stage or in a mock audition. Mental performance can be used simultaneously with polishing repertoire, mock auditions, and tapering before the audition, thus allowing the student to conserve vital energy.

MENTAL PERFORMANCE INSTRUCTIONS

Step 1: Get comfortable and Center
Mental performance begins with Centering. Find a comfortable position, lying down or sitting, making sure your back is straight. Place your hands over your center (imagining two inches below your navel and two inches towards your spine). Close your eyes, and take time to Center yourself. In addition to taking several slow deep breaths, check and release all muscle tension from head to toe. Breathe consciously into your center until you are in a state of physical relaxation and mental quiet.

Step 2: Imagine your flawless performance
After taking several Centering breaths, imagine walking confidently into the performance space. Imagine your pre-shot routine. Imagine performing the entire piece just the way you would like it to go: hear it clearly, feel it fully, and vividly see an amazing performance. Imagine walking proudly out of the room, knowing you did your best.

Step 3: Transition
Each time you are mentally performing an audition, challenge yourself by shifting the order of the pieces. This reveals possible tricky transitions between the required works (i.e., slow to fast, high to low, loud to soft, etc.).

Step 4: Reflect on your mental performance
Until you can imagine your mental performance going well, it will not

go as well as possible. If you are making mental mistakes, you need to return to mental practice to correct them as soon as possible.

TRUE STORY

Several years ago I worked with a 17-year-old violinist from the East Coast. She had great practice habits and always played well in her weekly lessons. Her dream was to be accepted into Juilliard. Unfortunately, she had not auditioned well at some of the other top schools to which she had applied. After talking with her, we discovered that she just could not imagine auditioning well in front of highly esteemed teachers.

She needed to learn how to mentally perform the upcoming Juilliard audition just the way she needed it to go. We started with the basics, with her imagining performing on stage at a top music school without anyone present. When she was able to vividly see, hear, and feel herself doing well there, we moved her mental performance to the Juilliard stage. After mentally performing well there without any teachers, she started adding them to her visualization, one by one, until the entire violin faculty was there. After she was able to vividly imagine performing well for them many times over, she was ready for the audition. She was admitted and enrolled at The Juilliard School.

from Don Greene

It will take less than 20 minutes a day for one week to make dramatic improvements in your ability to mentally perform and begin seeing yourself audition just the way you want.

BUILDING CONFIDENCE

There are three simple strategies to build confidence before an audition. The first is adequate and proper preparation. The second is daily mental performance. The third is positive self-talk: what the student is thinking before and during the time they are playing or singing.

Students: Here is an exercise to improve your confidence. It is simple but very powerful: Write out everything that you said to yourself while you were playing or singing today that you would not say to a good friend ("That was horrible, can't you do any better than that?") Next, write out what you would say instead to your friend ("Hang in there, you can do it.") Then, start practicing positive self-talk both in and out of the practice room. Confidence drops dramatically with self-criticism and increases significantly with positive reinforcement, like "You can do it!" or "Way to go!"

By following and working through all the parts of this chapter, confidence in one's ability to perform well during the college audition process will improve. It is impossible to anticipate all the variables that may occur during the process, but knowing they will be there and preparing for many of them will lead to successful auditions. In addition, Centering and mental performance are strategies that students can use throughout their careers.

THE AUDITION DAY:
Before and After

8

Between January and March of their senior year, most music performance-bound students will be taking more back-to-back auditions than ever before. Every audition will be different, but it is the student's goal to peak, or have a great performance, at each audition. As musicians move through their careers, they will find they are often at different playing levels and in different mental spaces depending on the day. However, some elements remain the same from audition to audition. These include how to handle travel, what to eat, and what to pack. Being very organized and prepared for a series of auditions will eliminate many travel-related variables, thus reducing stress.

ORGANIZING AUDITION TRAVEL

CREATE A CALENDAR OF AUDITION-RELATED DATES AND DEADLINES

A music school applicant must manage multiple deadlines. In addition to all the application and financial aid paperwork, which have their own deadlines, there are also prescreening recording deadlines, audition dates, and associated travel plans. It is recommended to create a calendar for the entire senior year, to help organize all the important dates and deadlines.

Because auditions take place in person at the school or at a regional site, choosing audition dates should be done strategically. There are many variables that must be taken into consideration when music students have to travel to an audition. These may include crossing time zones, jet lag, weather issues, altitude changes, mode of travel, etc. Parents and students may find that certain dates work well if the student is taking multiple auditions in the same city or same region of the country.

The applicant will often be asked to indicate audition date preferences on the application. Pencil in all the audition date options on the calendar. Plan to arrive in the city a minimum of twenty-four hours ahead of the scheduled audition, and include this in the calendar too. It is almost impossible to make every date fit perfectly, so if a conflict comes up, make sure to discuss this with the admissions office.

MAKE A PACKING LIST FOR AUDITION TRAVEL

- ☐ Instrument
- ☐ All instrument supplies (rosin, oil, repair tools, mouthpiece, mutes and practice mutes, etc.) *Double reed players: pack blades,*

screwdrivers, etc. in your checked suitcase which goes under the plane in cargo. If you only have a carry-on, leave most tools at home.

- ☐ Repertoire Binder/music
- ☐ Contact information for the school's admissions office
- ☐ Pen and pencil
- ☐ Comfortable travel clothes
- ☐ Nice audition day attire (include extra layers for cold climates)
- ☐ Snacks and water bottle
- ☐ Device to listen to music and headphones (Even if the auditioner is not listening to anything, people are less likely to bother someone who is wearing headphones.)
- ☐ Lip balm for wind and brass players
- ☐ Piano part(s) for accompanist (if necessary)
- ☐ Passport/Driver's license
- ☐ Directions to campus

WHAT IS APPROPRIATE AUDITION ATTIRE?

Remember that when you apply to college, you are starting your career. Make sure to dress in a way that says you are a potential professional, but that also is comfortable enough for a day of standing, sitting, and auditioning.

Dress pants/skirt and dress shirt are best. (No tuxedos, ball gowns, short skirts, jeans, shirts with words, tank tops, tennis shoes, spike heels, flip-flops, etc.)

PLAN AHEAD – SPECIAL REMINDERS TO THE APPLICANT

- Make sure you know exactly where the building, audition room, and check-in table are located before you arrive. Consult a map beforehand. If you have time the day before the audition, travel to the audition site to learn your way around.

- Prior to traveling, double-check your personal schedule for the audition day. There may be multiple parts to the audition day beside your audition (interview, placement tests, etc.). Since each school has a different schedule, knowing this information will get you in the right frame of mind for the day.

- Know the time of your first appointment, and arrive at least thirty minutes prior to that time.

- Find out if a warm-up room is provided. Sometimes practice rooms are not available for applicants because they are in use by current students. Sometimes the warm-up room is just one large, open space for multiple instruments. If there is no warm-up space provided for applicants, plan to warm up before arriving on campus.

- Stay hydrated. Water is best, regardless of your instrument or voice type. Eat nutritious meals, get ample rest and sleep, wear appropriate clothing for the weather, maintain a positive state of mind in the present, and an optimistic outlook for the near future. Audition season is not a sprint, it's a marathon. If you feel run down and need to recover, take a break. Your auditions will go better when you are rested.

HANDLE UNEXPECTED TRAVEL COMPLICATIONS

The most common travel complications are health, weather, and transportation related. What if the student gets sick, or a flight is delayed?

- Stay calm.

- Contact the music admissions office. (That is why you should bring their phone number with you.) Tell them the situation. Discuss possible solutions with them.

TRUE STORY

We were holding our auditions at the Eastman School of Music in February, the same as always. We received a call in the Admissions Office from a frantic mother, saying that her son was halfway there, but he got stuck in an airport due to a snowstorm. Then we received a call from the student (because he had the Admissions Office contact information with him, as recommended above). He, too, was panicked. Although he would arrive that day, he would miss crucial testing and interviews. Our advice to him was to come straight to the school when he arrived. We would make sure his audition was rescheduled, and would fit in everything else around that.

As admissions professionals, we really have seen it all, so we weren't thrown by these phone calls. The audition committee was informed that the student was delayed due to travel complications, and that they would hear him later in the day. The testing that he missed was made up in the school library, proctored by a librarian. He was placed into a later interview group.

What was the upshot of all this? The student was admissible, regardless of the snowstorm, and he ended up enrolling in the school.

from Kathleen Tesar

A NOTE TO PARENTS

If financially possible, at least one parent should travel with their musician to auditions. (It is best if this is the calmer parent.) Navigating a new city can be daunting for most 17- and 18-year-olds, so it is helpful if the parent can focus on the logistics while the student focuses on the music. Make sure to save any sightseeing or visits with family or friends until after the audition. When budgeting for auditions, include the cost of the parent's travel, meals, and lodging.

During the audition day, parents should attend any parent-specific talks or orientations offered by the institution. Otherwise, parents should make it a point to remain in the background throughout the day, and to follow any school policies (such as waiting in an area designated for parents). Do not over-share information about your child with teachers, admissions staff, or other parents. A supportive but discreet parent will surely help their applicant have a greater chance of success.

HELPFUL HINT: ADVICE FOR THOSE WHO PLAY LARGE INSTRUMENTS

Audition travel is expensive, and even more so when the instrument in question is really big. It is helpful to know that many schools do make accommodations for this.

HARP AND DOUBLE BASS PLAYERS: Ask the school if there is an instrument available for the audition. If so, ask if it is possible to have some time with the instrument before the audition so that you can get used to it. If possible, plan your travel to arrive the day before for this purpose.

PIANISTS AND ORGANISTS: A music school generally has excellent grand pianos for the audition, but you may not have access to the audition piano before the audition. To anticipate this, in the months prior to the audition, try out your material on as many different grand pianos in as many different spaces as you can. This will help you feel comfortable sitting down at an unknown instrument, in a large or small room. For the same reason, organists and harpsichordists should inquire about the audition instrument, and prepare by performing on different instruments in the months prior to auditions.

PERCUSSIONISTS: A typical percussion audition requires the applicant to play snare drum, marimba, and timpani. (You can confirm this by looking at the school's repertoire list.) The instruments are provided by the school, but don't count on having access to them prior to the audition. Bring your own mallets and sticks. Like pianists, you can anticipate this situation by practicing on different instruments prior to the audition, so that you get used to adjusting in the moment.

THE DAYS LEADING UP TO THE AUDITION

The days before the audition are all about your energy, and conserving that energy for the audition. Your performance will be affected by what you eat, how much travel you have to do, and how much sleep you get. Make sure that you increase your sleep time in the days before the audition. The most important night of sleep for any performance is two nights prior to the performance. Yes, there is school and homework and socializing, but sleep is one of the key elements to factor in before the audition. If you have trouble falling asleep, use the Centering process to relax the body and quiet the mind. If it is not possible to fall asleep right away, think about a happy memory or trip with friends until drifting off. Remember, you still get 70% of the rest value of sleep just by finding a comfortable position and lying there quietly.

Hydration is another immensely valuable element. Travel and stress can take a toll, and water replenishes the body. How do you know if you are drinking enough water? Not to put too fine a point on it, your urine will be clear instead of yellow. If it is clear, then you are drinking enough water. Do not try to cram water intake. Begin to increase your intake about 72 hours in advance of the audition, and slow down water intake about two hours before the audition. Some singers and wind and brass players may wish to take a water bottle into the audition with them. It depends on the instrumental or voice teacher at the school, but most are okay with this. (It should be noted, though, that auditions usually last only about ten minutes or so. Stopping to sip water during that brief period decreases the amount of time that a committee has to listen to an applicant.)

Another factor is travel plans. Whether you are driving or flying or using some other mode of transportation, if at all possible arrive 24 hours in advance of the audition. (Red-eye flights are not recommended!) This gives you some time in which to acclimate, practice, and sleep. The time also can be used to scope out where you need to be for the audition.

For food, keep it simple. It is recommended to stay away from salt and processed food, because they will make the tongue swell. (This is particularly undesirable for singers and wind and brass players.) Also avoid high-acidic foods, such as citrus fruit and tomatoes. Eating more potassium will slow down the adrenalin. Bananas are a good source of potassium, as are cantaloupe, lima beans, and potatoes; try eating some of these foods about 45 minutes before the audition. If you drink caffeine as part of your daily routine, do not change this routine. If you do not usually drink caffeine, do not start now, even to overcome jetlag. Caffeine speeds up the heart rate, and that is not a good thing going into an audition. Any meal prior to the actual performance should be fairly simple, but balanced with proteins and carbohydrates.

TYPES OF AUDITIONS

There are many variations in how music schools run their audition day. Always remember that the application process is an exchange of information, and that each school wants to know different things about their applicants. This accounts for many of the different approaches one can find in the way audition days are organized. One school may have a very simple audition process, while another school may have a very complicated one. Here are some of the extremes.

THE SIMPLE AUDITION DAY

The simple audition day boils down to, "I came, I performed, I left." In some cases, the approach is so simple that there is no one to greet the applicant when he or she arrives at the music building, no one to wish the applicant well afterward, and only a few signs (if any!) indicating where to go and what to do.

A school may have this kind of audition day for several reasons. Perhaps the school is very small, and the audition is for the applied teacher only (not a committee). The small school may not have the staff necessary for a more involved audition day. Or perhaps admission is based on academics and the audition is only to determine a music scholarship. A simple audition day may serve the school's purpose without the need for a more elaborate process.

THE COMPLEX AUDITION DAY

A school may choose to have a complex audition day for reasons opposite those cited above. If the faculty is large and auditions are heard by committees, scheduling can be a nightmare for the admissions staff, so there will be multiple activities going on in separate locations at the same time. If there is also a large number of applicants, it is easier to have big audition days with lots of activities. What are some activities on a complex audition day?

- The audition itself
- A theory or keyboard placement test (not for admission, but to "place" someone in the appropriate level of theory or keyboard class once enrolled)
- A campus tour
- An information session about the school or music department
- A session for parents
- A personal interview

DIG DEEPER: AUDITION DAY SCHEDULES

Here are some examples of complex audition days:

- http://cim.edu/conservatory/admission/audition-live
- http://www.esm.rochester.edu/admissions/ugrad/process/ (scroll down to "Audition Options")
- https://www.colburnschool.edu/conservatory/apply-to-the-conservatory/audition-los-angeles/ (click on "Audition Day Overview")

Some schools have student guides who help applicants find their way around on audition days. If these are current students, take advantage of the opportunity to ask them about the school, the facilities, and the teachers.

No matter what, remember that an audition day is an exchange of information. The applicant should use the visit to check out the school, but never forget that they are being assessed the entire time.

LIVE AUDITIONS AT A REGIONAL SITE

Some schools offer regional auditions. These are in-person auditions that are held off-campus, usually in larger cities. Typically, faculty are not present. Instead, a representative from the school will record the audition to send it back to the professor and the admissions committee. Bear in mind that in some cases it may be a disadvantage to audition off-campus, because the teacher is not present. An on-campus audition is always the better choice. Schools tend to assess the applicant's interest level based in part on whether they actually come to the institution to audition.

Before scheduling a regional audition, applicants should check with the faculty members or the admissions office at the institution to ensure that scholarship eligibility is the same at regional sites as on campus.

ROADMAP FOR LIVE AUDITIONS

Here is a great roadmap to follow, whether faced with a complex audition day, a simple audition day, or a regional audition:

1. Eat a simple but nutritious breakfast.
2. After breakfast, take a 15-20 minute walk. Breathe deeply. Imagine great sounds.

3. Arrive early at the audition site to allow time to warm up.

4. Read the signs, check in, and verify the day's schedule.

5. Locate the audition room.

6. Warm up.

7. Center.

8. Wait patiently outside the audition room five minutes before the scheduled time, or when directed by staff.

RECORDED AUDITIONS

Similar to regional auditions, some schools allow applicants to submit recorded auditions. These are similar to prescreening recordings because they are recorded by the applicant. However, recorded auditions usually involve more repertoire than prescreening recordings. The same caution applies to recorded auditions as to regional auditions: Since the recording is made by the applicant, without the presence of faculty or staff, there is no interaction like there would be at an in-person audition. Also some scholarship funds may be unavailable to applicants who submit audition recordings.

The cost of traveling to auditions can be steep, so recorded auditions can seem like a good idea. In general, if the budget is limited, then prioritize schools and be sure to travel to the applicant's top choice schools.

POST-AUDITION SELF-EVALUATION

When the applicant has finished playing the audition, only one task remains. Within thirty minutes of walking out of the audition room, the applicant should write down all of the things that went well and all of the things that could be improved for the next audition. Once this is written down, the audition is finally over. Do not overthink this. Wait a few days to review the post-audition notes, then begin to incorporate these ideas into preparation for the next audition.

POST-AUDITION PARENT ADVICE

For parents accompanying a child to an audition, here is the best question to ask the student after the audition: "Where do you want to go to eat?" It is best to leave the post-audition assessment to the student and their mentor.

AUDITION EVALUATION STRATEGY

Recording your live audition as you play will give you direct feedback later. Bring in a discreet recording device, turn it on before you enter the room. Forget that it exists. Then take it with you when you leave. Wait at least twenty-four hours before listening to your audition and, when possible, listen with your teacher. In evaluating this audition recording, you will likely make observations in two ways: You will start to identify your tendencies under pressure (for example, unsteady rhythm, not enough dynamic contrast, inconsistent intonation, etc.). You also might notice that your audition went better than you thought it did!

POST-AUDITION RECOVERY AND REWARDS

The timing of college auditions can be one of the biggest challenges in a student's life: auditions usually follow the winter holiday break, and travel can be affected by winter weather. Some students need to miss school and will have to make up work. When a student finishes an audition, no matter what is coming next, it is important to take a day to rest and recover. This may mean a day of light practice or even an entire day of staying away from singing or playing the instrument. Take some time to sleep, rest, and reboot.

Rewards are a very important part of the audition process. Students should make sure to give themselves at least one reward for finishing the audition. No matter how one feels after performing, a reward is important for the psyche. The student has just put in many hours of preparation; a tangible treat is appropriate (this does not need to be expensive). Many students like to purchase something for their case or practice room to symbolize the hard work and courage required to do well at the audition.

ADMISSION DECISIONS

9

There are three possible decisions that a college can make regarding an application: "accept," "deny," or "waitlist." The sections below describe what each means, and what is required of the applicant in each circumstance.

THE OFFER OF ADMISSION

"Congratulations, you have been accepted!" An applicant's obligations do not end with the offer of admission. There are quite a few ethical considerations attached to this step, for both the institution and the applicant. There are also a lot of factors to consider before an applicant accepts the offer.

The first thing to note is that an offer of admission is not official unless it comes from the school's designated admissions officer. No matter how enthusiastic the faculty members are at an audition or interview, the offer is only real is when it comes from the person whose job it is to admit students to the institution. An enthusiastic teacher may offer very encouraging words to the student during the audition, but "I'd like you to be in my studio," is NOT an offer of admission.

Therefore, one of the first ethical considerations is that the school must send the applicant an official offer of admission, as a hard copy letter, by email, or by accessing the applicant's record in the university's application database. This official offer of admission may be accompanied by other documents such as financial aid information, enrollment forms, and even housing information, all of which must be reviewed and understood.

Applicants will be given instructions for responding and a deadline. For undergraduate music majors, offers of admission are sent around April 1, and the deadline to respond is May 1. The system is set up so that the applicant and their family have about a month to examine all offers of admission, discuss the factors that go into making the decision (cost, location, teacher, program, etc.), and arrive at a wise and informed decision. Applicants are specifically encouraged NOT to commit to a school until all factors have been considered. Applicants to graduate music programs generally are notified earlier and have an April 15 deadline to respond. Once a school has made an offer of admission, it cannot withdraw the offer before the response deadline unless unethical behavior on the part of the applicant is discovered.

An applicant is obligated to respond to every offer of admission— even if the applicant is declining the offer. For every offer of admission that is declined, a school can offer admission to a waitlisted applicant. Admissions officers anticipate a percentage of declines, so once an applicant has decided, that decision must be conveyed to all of the schools by the stated deadlines, if not sooner. In the music world, it is an appropriate gesture for a student who declines an offer of admission to send a note or email to the applied professor with whom they would have studied (see Appendix 13).

DIG DEEPER: MAKING A DECISION

The National Association for College Admission Counseling (NACAC) provides a quick overview of the applicant's enrollment decision process: https://www.nacacnet.org/globalassets/documents/publications/collegebreakdown.pdf.

DENIAL OF ADMISSION

The denial of admission can be painful, but every denial opens up a different path. Sometimes being denied admission is a relief; sometimes it is heartbreaking—both for the applicant and the parent. Here are two things to remember:

- Denial of admission is only for that one application; it is not for future applications. Sometimes students are admitted on a second or even a third application (as transfer applicants for example), or for graduate study instead of undergraduate study.

- The applicant has no way of knowing why the denial of admission occurred. It is all too easy for a young musician to imagine the worst, and to internalize a message that does not exist. Factors beyond the applicant's control may be in play. Examples of these factors include the number of applicants, the number of openings, and the level of the other applicants. Therefore, it is a waste of energy to speculate on why an applicant was denied admission.

Once the student learns that a specific school has denied admission, it is time to move on, focus on the other schools, and rearrange one's thinking to accept the new reality.

WAITLIST WHYS AND HOWS

Being placed on a school's waitlist can be uncomfortable and confusing because the applicant has not been denied admission, but has not been offered admission either. The applicant is not in, and is not out. How does this work?

An admissions officer at a music school is tasked with making sure that when the new academic year starts, the school has enough musicians to fulfill its mission. An orchestra cannot exist with 20 flutes and 4 violins; a choir cannot have 15 tenors and 2 basses. An orchestral cellist who never played in orchestra because there were too many other cellists has not received proper training. Waitlists are used to manage enrollment. This benefits the institution and the students, because having the proper enrollment balances the student body so that training is appropriate and effective.

VOCABULARY: WAITLISTS

This is how the National Association of College Admission Counseling defines **WAITLISTS**:

"Waitlist is an admission decision option utilized by institutions to protect against shortfalls in enrollment, in light of fluctuations in yields. By placing a student on the waitlist, an institution does not initially offer or deny admission, but extends to the candidate the possibility of admission not later than August 1."

—from NACAC's Statement of Principles of Good Practice, II.B.6.a (approved by the 2014 Assembly)

Here is the most important point about waitlists: **If an undergraduate applicant on a waitlist at a specific school has not received an offer of admission from that school by April 30, the applicant must commit to enrolling in a different school (that has admitted them) by May 1.**

From the institution's perspective, the school has made offers of admission, denied admission, and has created a waitlist. After May 1, the school is no longer obligated to hold the place offered to an accepted applicant who has not responded. In other words, after May 1 the school assumes that any applicant who has not responded is declining the offer of admission; the school is then free to offer admission to applicants on their waitlist. (Note: A school is never obligated to admit applicants from the waitlist.)

It is recommended for an applicant on a waitlist to contact the admissions office and ask, "Where am I on the waitlist?" Some schools do not "rank" students on the waitlist; however, those that do will normally report the number. In addition, schools will ask waitlisted applicants, "Do you wish to remain on the waitlist?" It is recommended to stay on a school's waitlist until the applicant is positive that they would not want to go to that school even if they got accepted (see Appendix 14).

The problem from the admissions office side is that waitlists are very changeable. If there are ten applicants on the undergraduate horn waitlist on April 30, the school assumes that all ten will make commitments to other institutions (because of the May 1 response deadline for undergraduates). Then when the school has an opening and calls one of these waitlisted applicants, it is possible that the applicant may not wish to consider a late offer. This means that the number two applicant on the waitlist is now number one. The applicant who is number eight out of ten may conclude that there is no chance of an offer, but many schools will run through a large number of waitlisted applicants to fill an open position. Therefore, the wisest course for any applicant is to remain on the waitlist, unless certain they do not want to attend. Schools may call any time up to August 1 with an offer, and one never knows what may happen over the summer.

(Note that this advice to remain on a waitlist is more applicable to music students than to non-music majors. If a flute waitlist has ten or fifteen applicants on it, one can assume that they are all admissible but that there are not enough flute openings. This is different from a liberal arts school, for example, where there may be one hundred or even one thousand applicants on the waitlist, and therefore the odds of being admitted off the waitlist are smaller.)

If an applicant has accepted an offer from another school, and is 100% committed to where the enrollment deposit was paid, it is a professional courtesy to tell the school where the applicant is waitlisted that they are no longer interested, as this has a domino effect of helping the school and the other applicants who remain on the waitlist.

How is this late (post-May 1) offer handled, if all applicants had to make commitments to other schools by then?

The school with the opening contacts the applicant on the waitlist. The school asks two questions:

1. Is the waitlisted applicant interested in considering an offer of admission?

2. If so, has the applicant committed to another school? (If it is after May 1, the school understands that it is very likely that the applicant has indeed made a commitment somewhere.)

This exchange is NOT an offer of admission!

These same questions are asked whether the offer is being made to a waitlisted applicant prior to or after May 1. In both cases, the school with the opening will contact the school where the applicant has paid a deposit *before making an official offer to the applicant*, as a courtesy to the other school, and as required by the National Association of Schools of Music (the accrediting body for most music programs). Once the other school is informed (and possibly has acknowledged the contact in writing), the school with the opening can proceed with the offer. An applicant who is waitlisted at their top choice school is advised to hold off making a deposit elsewhere until April 30, but (as noted above) making sure to enroll somewhere by May 1.

While this process may seem quite convoluted on the institutional side, it ensures communication between admissions offices, and prevents misunderstandings institutionally. The chief admissions officers at peer schools in the music world often know each other professionally, and have worked to build good relationships. Those relationships help a great deal when it comes to these waitlist calls.

One question that always arises from waitlisted applicants is, "How much financial aid will I be offered from the institution that originally waitlisted me?" This answer will vary from institution to institution and circumstance to circumstance. It is wise to begin this discussion as soon as the offer is made. Do not withdraw from the institution to which the student has committed until receiving a full financial aid package as well as the official offer of admission from the previously waitlisted school.

If a student decides to accept an offer from the school where they were waitlisted and to withdraw from the school where they had enrolled, they should notify the admissions office and also write to the applied teacher to let them know of the new decision (see Appendix 14).

FINANCIAL AID

10

Earlier in this book it was stated that the cost of a school should NOT be a factor in deciding where to apply. However, it most certainly IS a factor in deciding where to enroll. The key point here is that the final cost of the school may bear no resemblance to the posted cost, and an applicant will not know the final cost until the financial aid package is received.

TRUE STORY

A young woman from a small city in Georgia applied to Georgia State University because she qualified for in-state tuition. She also took a chance and applied to Harvard. She was admitted to both schools but thought she could never attend Harvard because the tuition was much more expensive. However, when she sat down with her family to examine all of the decision factors, Harvard turned out to cost less than Georgia State! If she had limited herself to in-state schools because of the posted "sticker price," she never would have had the opportunity to attend Harvard—which she did, and she is now embarking on graduate work at Yale.

from Kathleen Tesar

First, some big-picture thoughts: If an individual has the goal of attending college, then paying for it is part of their responsibility. The government provides loans and grants to students and their families who qualify in order to help them reach this goal. Individual institutions have their own policies about merit aid and scholarships, and there are independent sources of scholarships and loans. The authors of this book are not financial aid officers or tax advisors. What is offered here is information about the whys and hows of aid, along with links to resources to help families make sense of this part of the process.

DIG DEEPER: FINANCIAL AID

Here is what Swarthmore College has to say (http://www.swarthmore.edu/admissions-aid/financial-aid-and-cost-information)—

> "Although we believe that the primary responsibility for financing education lies with students and their parents or guardians, we stand ready to help fill in the gap when family resources do not meet our costs. Swarthmore's strong financial aid program demonstrates our commitment to the principle that all capable students have access to the College."

ONLINE RESOURCES

Many websites exist to help families figure out aid for college study. Official websites of the U.S. government end in ".gov." These sites are updated often and provide solid information; visit these websites first. Here are some short descriptions of useful websites, starting with one related to the cost of college:

https://nces.ed.gov/ - The National Center for Education Statistics (NCES) collects and analyzes data related to education in the U.S. One of the ways it gathers data is through IPEDS—the Integrated Postsecondary Education Data System. Since completion of IPEDS surveys is required of any post-secondary institution that receives federal Title IV funding, this website is an incredible source of information. College Navigator is one of the tools provided by NCES. It can be used to get information on specific schools. The "general information" tab on a school's record includes a link directly to the school's net price calculator. For example, by entering "Curtis Institute of Music," this page of information appears: http://nces. ed.gov/collegenavigator/?q=curtis+institute+of+music&s=all&id=211893.

https://studentaid.ed.gov/types - This website from the U.S. Department of Education describes sources of aid: the federal government, the state in which the student lives, the college itself, and nonprofit or private organizations. It goes further and lists other government resources, such as aid for serving in the military, tax benefits, etc.

http://financialaidtoolkit.ed.gov/tk/ - This is another website from the U.S. Department of Education, packed full of information for students, parents, counselors, and mentors. It includes this handy "College Preparation Checklist" that focuses on college planning with an emphasis on federal student aid: https://studentaid.ed.gov/sites/default/files/college-prep-checklist.pdf.

https://fafsa.ed.gov/ - "FAFSA" stands for "Free Application for Federal Student Aid." This application is the *only way* to apply for U.S. government money. Even if the family is unsure whether they qualify for federal aid, the student should still fill out this application because it may lead to other types of aid or scholarship.

HELPFUL HINT: PLAN AHEAD FOR FINANCIAL AID DATES AND DEADLINES

The FAFSA is the Free Application for Federal Student Aid; completing this form gives families access to federal aid for attending college. The government makes the FAFSA available beginning on October 1. The aid itself is disbursed by the school in which the student enrolls. For example, a student needing aid to attend school in the fall of 2019 can start the FAFSA as early as October 2018. The tax return used will be the FAFSA from the 2017 calendar year.

Make sure you check your state and school financial aid deadlines. Some states award aid on a first-come, first-served basis, so you are encouraged to complete the FAFSA as soon as possible. In addition, it is always best to check the websites of all your schools to know their financial aid deadlines. For example, Cal Grants for California public institutions are due on March 2. Some private school deadlines may be even sooner. You can start a calendar with financial aid deadlines the summer before the senior year of high school. The best advice here is KNOW THE DEADLINES.

https://student.collegeboard.org/css-financial-aid-profile - This is not a federal website, but many schools require students to complete the CSS Profile in addition to the FAFSA. The CSS Profile is for non-federal financial aid. Schools that require both the FAFSA and the Profile are looking for a multi-dimensional understanding of the family's financial situation before offering aid. Check with the school to know if the CSS Profile is required.

http://www.careerinfonet.org/scholarshipsearch/ - This website is sponsored by the U.S. Department of Labor, and provides a search tool for scholarships as well as information on careers, training, and job searches.

http://www.fastweb.com/ - Fastweb is not a federal website, but it is a great resource for college planning. Their educator page has download-able information: http://www.fastweb.com/content/download_free_ materials, including tips on filling out the FAFSA. They have articles on applying to college: http://www.fastweb.com/college-search/articles/, and information on scholarships not related to specific institutions. They even have a page on scholarship themes: http://www.fast-web.com/college-scholarships/scholarship-themes/articles. Fastweb scholarships tend to hit the extremes—scholarships with criteria so broad that everyone qualifies, or so narrow that almost no one qualifies (National Potato Council Scholarship anyone? It's worth $10,000.)— but the writing on the website is clear and understandable, and it's all free. You should never pay to find a scholarship.

TRUE STORY

One motivated flute player, fearing his family would not be able to afford the type of school he wanted to attend, started applying for scholarships the summer before his senior year. He applied to his father's employer, to the local music club, to WalMart—everywhere he could find. In the end, his efforts resulted in a total of $20,500 from multiple sources, most granted in amounts under $2,000.

from Kathleen Tesar

TYPES OF AID

The job of the school's financial aid office is to enroll the entering class while staying within the school's financial aid budget. In addition to this budget, the financial aid office has to abide by the institutional policies and federal regulations for awarding aid. There are some key differences between federal aid and institutional aid.

FEDERAL AID

This money does not belong to the school. Rather, the school passes the money along from the U.S. government to the student. A school must be approved by the federal government to handle this money, and that means the school has the burdens of both accountability and obligation. *Accountability* means the school must meet federal requirements for handling the funds, including maintaining accreditation in good standing, having adequate financial aid staffing, and undergoing regular audits to determine compliance. *Obligation* means they are required to report data and follow certain federal policies in return for participating in federal programs. (Examples of this include completing the IPEDS survey mentioned above, and obeying FERPA, the Solomon Act, the Clery Act, etc.) The awarding of federal funds is based on the FAFSA, not on the school's philosophy. Types of federal aid include loans, grants, and work-study. Loans have to be paid back; grants do not.

VOCABULARY: WORK-STUDY

WORK-STUDY is the government's way of subsidizing student employment. Therefore, the less the school has to spend on paying student workers, the more money it has to fund other institutional aid. The student still has to find a job, be hired, and actually work in order to earn the money; work-study is not a grant.

As an example, a student worker is hired for an on-campus job that pays $10 an hour. Normally, that would cost the school $10 an hour. However, if the job is a work-study job, then part of that $10 an hour is paid by the federal government, thus saving the institution some of the cost of hiring the student.

INSTITUTIONAL AID

Institutional aid is money in the school's financial aid budget that is not funded by the government, and thus its distribution is determined by the school's financial aid philosophy and policies. Types of institutional aid include grants and scholarships.

When the institution's financial aid office puts together an aid package for an admitted applicant, it is partly a question of plugging in the applicant's data (to determine how much and what kind of aid they qualify for) and partly a question of institutional policy (lots of aid to a top applicant, an even amount of aid for all applicants, or other criteria). There is also the factor of musical requirements. For example, if the applicant pool for bassoon was particularly small, then the school may need to offer more aid to enroll bassoon students, and that may result in less aid for violin students.

UNDERSTANDING FINANCIAL AID PACKAGES

When the financial aid award letter arrives, initial excitement may be followed by confusion: How does one make sense of this? The confusion is often a result of how the cost of the institution is defined and the different types of aid being awarded to help offset that cost.

The cost to attend a school is more than just tuition. Tuition covers instruction, but there are also charges for books, room and board, fees (comprehensive, student life, technology, etc.), and health insurance. Aid includes both grants and scholarships that do not need to be repaid and loans that do. Room and board fees are typically not included in financial aid packages. If they are included, the government considers the amounts to be taxable income. If a "full ride" is offered to an applicant, it is very important to verify whether that refers to having tuition covered, or if the award goes beyond tuition (and subsequently may have tax consequences).

The charges posted on a school's website are not the final amount that a student pays. Some costs can only be estimated at the time of enrollment. Other costs are variable, such as the fee for a single room versus the fee for a double (shared) room. The award letter defines the particular mix of loans, grants, and scholarships that a specific school is offering to a specific student to cover the cost of attendance. Award letters also may estimate the family's contribution (known as the "EFC," or "estimated family contribution").

Here are some resources to help decipher the award letter and financial aid package:

- http://www.fastweb.com/nfs/fastweb/static/QRG_FinancialAid AwardLetters.pdf
- http://www.finaid.org/fafsa/awardletters.phtml

- http://www.financialaidsense.com/financial-aid-articles/
award-letters/financial-aid-award-letter-comparison

Once a student knows the final cost of an institution, it is then possible to compare costs across different schools.

TRUE STORY

A music applicant met a faculty member after an audition. The professor told him that he would be admitted and would receive a very generous scholarship. When the official offer of admission arrived—without notice of the scholarship—the student wanted to send in his enrollment deposit immediately. The mother asked him to wait until a letter confirming the scholarship arrived. No letter ever arrived. After repeated calls to the dean of the music school, the mother learned that the scholarship money had been offered to another applicant (who played an instrument that was more needed than her child's instrument). Thanks to a cautious parent, the family avoided making a commitment based on incomplete information.

from Kathleen Tesar

MAKING AN APPEAL

The applicant's dream has come true: An offer of admission and a financial aid package from the number one school has arrived. The family sits down to crunch the numbers, and finds that they cannot afford to have the student enroll in that school. The student can decline the offer of admission, or appeal for more aid. If the student declines the offer of admission, that is it. The school will admit the next person on the waitlist. There is no going back. If the school is the applicant's number one choice, however, it is worth contacting the school before declining the offer. Here are some things to understand before making an appeal.

The music school usually has a pool of scholarship money to distribute to students. As of April 1, the music school usually has awarded most of that money, leaving some for appeals. Once a student turns down an institution, that aid money returns to the music school's pool of scholarship money. If it is a university, the money may go back to the big institution's pool of money. In this case, the music department would have to request more money from that big institutional pool to use for appeals. The music department will want to do this only if they are certain that a student who has appealed will commit to that school if they offer more aid.

It is recommended that the family appeal as soon as possible after receiving the offer of admission and the financial aid package. The closer the May 1 response deadline, the busier the financial aid office will be, and the higher the likelihood that the scholarship budget will be spent.

Each institution has a different structure for the committee that awards aid. Some schools have committees that include the private teachers, while others include only department chairs (i.e., string chair, voice chair, winds/brass/percussion chair, etc.). Other institutions do not include any music faculty at all on the financial aid/scholarship committee. Because of this, applicants may want to keep their applied instructor(s) at the school in the loop regarding their appeal, in case the instructor has a voice on the committee. It is not the applicant's job to figure out the financial aid structure of every institution to which they were accepted; however, it is the applicant's job to be very clear about what they need in order to enroll.

In an appeal letter, include the following (see Appendix 15 for a sample letter):

1. This is the applicant's first choice of institution to attend. (Do not say this if it is not true.)

2. The reasons why the applicant wants to attend this particular institution.

3. An exact amount of additional aid needed per year in order for the applicant to attend.

4. Any information that will make the applicant's appeal stronger (e.g., I have four siblings who will all be enrolling in school soon, my parent is a single parent, there has been tragedy in the family, a family member is ill, I am supporting myself 100%, my parent is a free-lancer and their income varies, etc.).

Schools have different philosophies of awarding scholarship. Aid may be strategic, but it is not a contest, nor is it a sign of affection or lack thereof. Especially at very competitive schools, every admitted applicant merits scholarship. Therefore, in order for a school to determine whether to increase a financial aid or scholarship offer, the applicant needs to present a sincere, truthful, and concise justification for their appeal. If the cost of attending the applicant's top choice school is considerably beyond the applicant's ability to pay, the applicant may appeal to the school with a specific amount needed, but should also consider the possibility of attending another school. In the end, an applicant may appeal for more aid to several schools but always with the honest intention of enrolling should that appeal be granted.

Sometimes teachers or department chairs put pressure on applicants to commit or promise to enroll if they are offered more aid. The May 1 deadline protects undergraduate applicants from this pressure (and the same for the April 15 deadline for graduate applicants). Remember that an applicant is not committed to the school until the enrollment paperwork has been submitted.

A few final thoughts on appeals:

- Do not treat the appeal as an exercise in creative bargaining. The school is there to meet your need, not to offer you a bargain rate. Remember that financial aid officers are not used-car salesmen. They only have so much money in their budgets.

- If the school is the applicant's number one choice, say so. If it is not, do not lie.

- Avoid playing one school off another. Telling School B that School A gave the applicant more money will not convince a school to increase aid.

- Be specific about how much more aid is needed.

- After reviewing the financial aid packet and appealing, if you still cannot afford the school, be prepared to walk away.

TRUE STORY

In my years of teaching high school music students, I have helped many students find increased funding to attend their dream institution. I will share two stories with you.

Bryan's dream was to enroll as a music performance major in the school of music at a major university. He also applied to other schools, and was offered admission to both his dream school and his second choice school. The estimated cost of attendance (a number that includes tuition, room, board, books, etc.) at his dream school was over $72,000. The offer of aid was $5,000; his second-choice school offered almost full tuition. Both of Bryan's parents are employed, but the cost to attend his number one school put it beyond their reach. Bryan planned to enroll at his second-choice school, but tried one more appeal to his first-choice school prior to the May 1 response deadline. On April 30, at 4:50pm, Bryan's first choice school offered him $40,000 more, and he made his commitment to enroll there.

Susan was accepted to her first-choice school, but with a financial aid package of only $7,000 per year. Susan grew up without much money, the child of a single mom who could barely make ends meet. Despite the challenges, Susan worked hard at improving on her instrument. She was determined to major in music at her first-choice school, so she wrote a letter to the admissions office explaining why she needed a total of $25,000 per year to attend. The school was so moved by her letter that they increased her financial aid package to $30,000 and Susan enrolled.

from Annie Bosler

OTHER WAYS TO HELP PAY FOR COLLEGE

Each student needs to be prepared for all of the costs associated with attending college—not just tuition, room and board, and activities fees, but travel to and from school, clothing (especially concert attire), medical co-pays, prescription medicine, instrument maintenance, sheet music, recordings, and more. If the student does not have enough money in the bank, what can be done? Here are a few ideas that may be helpful.

- **Outside scholarships** are scholarships awarded by organizations other than the school itself. They must be reported to the school where the student enrolls, and they may reduce the amount of other aid. Examples include:
    - Fastweb, noted earlier in the chapter, is a good place to research outside scholarships.
        - http://www.fastweb.com/college-scholarships
    - Local Music Club Scholarships
        - https://atlantamusicclub.org/scholarships/
        - https://sbmusicclub.org/scholarship-info/
        - http://www.naplesmusicclub.org/scholarships/
    - Kiwanis Club scholarships
        - http://www.clubscholarships.us/kiwanis-scholarship/
- **Books**
    - *Secrets to Winning a Scholarship* (Mark Kantrowitz)
    - *Twisdoms* (Mark Kantrowitz)
    - *Confessions of a Scholarship Winner* (Kristina Ellis)
    - *Debt Free U: How I Paid for an Outstanding Education... without Loans, Scholarships, or Mooching Off My Parents* (Zac Bissonnette)
- **Part-time employment,** including work-study if awarded, is another source of income. This is a tough one for a student balancing studies and practicing, but a part-time job that relates to a student's musical interests can provide money, experience, and knowledge. Examples include stage crew, teacher's assistant, program notes writer, marketing assistant, usher, etc.

- **Resident Assistants (RAs)** are students who live in a school's residence hall and are members of the Residential Life staff. Students must apply for these positions, typically at the end of each academic year, and often receive a large reduction in the cost of room and board once they become RAs.

BASIC REMINDERS ABOUT AID

- A school cannot offer financial aid until the student has applied and been accepted.

- The only official offer of financial aid is the one that comes from the financial aid or admissions office. A statement by a faculty member that they want the applicant to receive a scholarship is NOT an official offer.

- Never sign an enrollment agreement without all of the financial facts. If an expected scholarship is not included in the offer, ask why it is not included. If the terms of a loan are unclear, ask for an explanation.

MUSIC CAREERS:
Motivation and Success

11

"Majoring in music" is often interpreted as becoming a performer or an educator, but there are many other career opportunities for a music major. Parents are often concerned about what a student will do with an undergraduate degree in music—to some parents the degree may seem impractical. The goal of this chapter is to broaden the picture by showing the many options available within music study, and also to highlight the many transferable skills that are developed by obtaining a degree in music.

Students choose careers in music out of love. They love singing or playing their instrument, performing or writing songs, or listening to all kinds of music. This emotional commitment sustains the energy required to pursue a creative path. Embarking on a career in music, there is no telling what new paths a student will find.

It is recommended that parents and students have a conversation about motivation. Why does the student want to major in music? What does it mean to them in terms of a career? What do they bring to their studies, and what do they need to take from them? Such a conversation can help steer the choices of where to apply.

Majoring in music develops a great many skills. Some of these skills are specific to a music career; many of them are much broader.

- Ability to prioritize
- Ability to work and communicate within a group
- Ability to work independently
- An understanding of excellence
- Artistic vocabulary and taste
- Competence
- Confidence in public speaking
- Creativity
- Focus
- Organizational skills
- Problem-solving skills
- Resilience
- Self-discipline
- Self-efficacy
- Self-regulation
- Stage presence
- Understanding of teamwork, accountability, and community
- Versatility

Majoring in music is the gateway to many career paths. As an exercise, take the word "music" and use it as an adjective, putting it in front of other professions: music therapy, music production, music law, music administration, music retail, music publishing, etc. There are hundreds of different careers within music. And within these broad categories there are even more professions. Here is a partial list; a more extensive list is available in Appendix 16:

- Audio Engineering (film music, television, theme parks, video games, pop artists, etc.)
- Arts Politics (music union or guild representative, National Endowment for the Arts, etc.)
- Composition (contemporary composer, film composer, orchestrator, songwriter, etc.)
- Conductor (orchestra, opera, film music, etc.)
- Marching Band (field show writer, drum corps instructor, etc.)
- Music Administration (symphony management, executive director, dean, etc.)
- Music Business (music agent, publicist, social media expert, etc.)
- Music Education (band director, music history teacher, music theory teacher, etc.)
- Music Law (entertainment lawyer, copyright specialist, etc.)
- Music Medicine (music therapist, performance psychology, research, etc.)
- Music Performance (orchestral musician, soloist, opera singer, studio musician, etc.)
- Music Preparation (orchestrator, copyist, librarian, etc.)
- Music Producer (music supervisor, contractor, engineer, etc.)
- Music Research (academic professor, historical music specialist, etc.)

- Music Sales/Retail (instrument maker, publishing, music store manager, etc.)

- Music Writer (music critic, music journalist, music historian, etc.)

- Physics of Music (acoustician, professor, etc.)

TRUE STORY

Ryan went to school to major in horn performance. After completing his undergraduate degree, Ryan began working as a dialogue editor. Because of his training in music, he developed great sensitivity to pitch, phrasing, and detail, as well as hearing the differences in sound timbre, color, and inflection. Ryan still plays horn in local community groups, but he has made a career editing dialogue for major network TV shows. He credits his unique career to his musical training.

from Annie Bosler

Often, students entering music programs only know they want to pursue the career path in music in general, but they have yet to decide on an area of specialization. That choice unfolds gradually as the student proceeds through their studies. This is similar to when a student decides to be a lawyer or a doctor, not knowing yet what their specialty will be. Some music students start out wanting to perform, so they enter their undergraduate degree as a performance major (not realizing all of the other options).

An undergraduate degree in music performance can be a great asset to anyone wanting to continue into other fields within the music industry. Classes in aural skills develop acute hearing, which is an asset in the recording industry, among other fields. Classes in music history develop research and writing skills, which are assets in any career. Knowing how to communicate effectively using musical terms can help to determine the quality of a musical product (such as when managing an orchestra). Thus music performance training creates stellar professionals within the music industry. Students should take advantage… in any direction.

DIG DEEPER: GRAMMY CAMP

Grammy Camp is a great way for high school students to explore other avenues outside of classical music performance. This summer program is held in Los Angeles with actual working professionals in the field. Check the website for more information: http://www.grammyintheschools.com/programs/grammy-camp. The areas to which a student may apply include:

> Audio Engineering
>
> Electronic Music Production
>
> Music Business
>
> Music Journalism
>
> Performance - Instrumental
>
> Performance - Vocal
>
> Songwriting
>
> Video Production & Motion Graphics

For a student wishing to major in an area such as audio engineering, electronic music production, music journalism, songwriting, video production, or motion graphics, Grammy Camp is a perfect opportunity to build a portfolio while receiving qualified faculty feedback. Often schools will want samples of a student's work to be submitted with the application. Grammy Camp is a perfect jumpstart for that type of portfolio.

Students who know that their career path is and always will be music performance should plan on making themselves as versatile as possible in today's world. There are skills that are important to every artist, whether majoring in performance or in another area of music: communication skills, marketing skills, an understanding of social media, website design, clear and concise writing, accounting and bookkeeping experience, contract negotiation, networking, ability to record oneself, photo and film editing, familiarity with music writing software, knowledge of business practices, etc. Some schools offer classes in these areas and others do not, but one can always find ways to learn and gain experience. For example, if a university student is interested in music business and a school's music program does not offer a business class, the student can enroll in a class or two through the business department. Interning is another great way to gain experience in the music industry.

TRUE STORY

I was in my Master of Music degree program at the University of Southern California majoring in horn performance. I knew I loved music and playing horn, but I did not know if I wanted an orchestra job for the rest of my life. During my years at USC, I decided to find internships in different areas of the music industry to see if there was a better fit for me. I interned in a new job each year: Public Relations at the Los Angeles Philharmonic, Marketing at the Los Angeles Chamber Orchestra, Music Supervision at Raleigh Studios in Hollywood, CA, and Artist Relations at the Spoleto Festival in Charleston, SC.

Through these different positions, I realized that a nine-to-five office job was not for me; however, I gained experience for my résumé and unique skills from each job that have served me well in my professional life. I went on to get a DMA in horn performance and now work as a professional freelance horn player and teacher in Los Angeles. I use these skills everyday.

from Annie Bosler

For the authors of this book, working in music has been an infinitely gratifying career choice. While each has taken a very different path, all three have had great success in the field of music.

The authors wish you great luck on your musical journey!

APPENDIX 1
Sample Email Requesting a Trial Lesson

Dear Professor [professor's last name],

My name is [your name]. I am currently a senior at [name of high school], and I study [instrument/voice] with [your teacher's full name] in [city, state]. [If you study in a pre-college or prep department, also include the name of that school.] I am interested in applying to [name of college/university/conservatory] for the fall of [year to start studying]. I am planning a trip to your city around [list dates or approximate timeframe]. Is it possible to schedule a lesson with you during that time?

Thank you for your time, and I look forward to hearing from you.

Sincerely,

[your name]
[your phone number]
[your email]

REMINDERS:

- Make sure you include your contact information, so the professor knows how to reach you.

- If you want to meet with the admissions office or take a campus tour, schedule those activities after the lesson is confirmed. Many admissions offices require a reservation for a campus tour and information session.

- Many schools allow faculty members to decide for themselves if they wish to meet with prospective students. If you ask for a lesson and are turned down, do not take it personally. It may simply mean that the professor is busy, or that they have a personal policy not to meet with prospective students.

- Choosing teachers and setting up lessons takes a lot of planning, so make sure you have lots of lead time to set up travel and confirm lesson times with the teachers.

- Because audition periods at schools can be very busy times for faculty, it is less likely that you will be able to have a lesson during auditions. However, at smaller schools, the audition itself may be more like a lesson.

- Finally, before you begin contacting applied teachers and requesting lessons, make sure that any videos of your playing that are posted on social media represent your current level of playing. Delete any old recordings, on the off chance that a teacher may look you up.

APPENDIX 2
Campus Visit Pros and Cons List

Campus tours are a great way for you to narrow down schools and get a feel for the campus and student life. If possible, try to schedule the tour while school is in session. The energy on campus is very different when students are present than when they are on a break.

Some schools require prospective students to make an appointment for a campus tour, while others may take walk-ins. Check the school's website or call the admissions office to inquire about campus tours.

Asking similar questions at each campus will help you have a better picture of the schools when making a final decision. It is recommended to keep a pros and cons list for each school. In other words, list the positives and and negatives in answer to each question. The following chart is an example of such a list of pros and cons, along with other suggestions of what to investigate during your campus visit:

	PROS	CONS
Campus: Take a tour of the campus.		
Residence Halls: Take a tour of the residence halls.		
Applied Teacher: Take a lesson with the instructor (or one of the instructors) in your major. Did you enjoy this person's teaching style and way of communicating? (Make sure to schedule this well in advance of your actual visit to campus.) Does the applied teacher commute from a long distance or do they live nearby? (This could affect how often you see the teacher.)		
Professors: Try to meet some of the professors—not just applied teachers, but teachers of music history, music theory, liberal arts, etc. Are the professors active in their fields?		

	PROS	CONS
Size: How big is the department/studio (that is, how many cello students if you are a cellist, or how many guitarists if you're a guitarist)?		
Lessons & Ensembles: Are you required to take lessons and/or play in ensembles to graduate? How many different ensembles are there and which ones interest you?		
Students: Try to meet several students within your major or department. Are they performing in their preferred ensembles? Can you see yourself hanging out and working with these people?		

	PROS	CONS
Track Record: What are graduates of this program, department, and/or school doing? (i.e., Where are they going to grad school? Where are they working? Are they successfully making a living in music? etc.)		
Music Curriculum: Does the curriculum cover the areas of music that interest you? (Visit the school's website to see course requirements and electives.)		
Auditions: Is there a beginning-of-the-year audition (such as for ensemble seating)?		
Non-Music Curriculum: What classes are available to you outside of music?		
Summer Internships and Festivals: What percentage of the student body is attending a summer festival or holding an internship?		

	PROS	CONS
Area Surrounding School: What is the area or town like just outside of campus? How easy is it to get around?		
Comfort Level: Do you feel a sense of "home" when you are on campus?		

For more questions to add to your list, see Chapter 4, "Asking the Right Questions."

APPENDIX 3
Lists of Post-Secondary Programs and Majors

Undergraduate degree programs related to music study have different names. When we did our research, here are the degree names that we found:

- Bachelor of Arts (BA)
- Bachelor of Fine Arts (BFA)
- Bachelor of Music (BM)
- Bachelor of Science (BS)
- Bachelor of Arts in Music (BAM)
- Bachelor of Interdisciplinary Studies (BIS)
- Bachelor of Musical Arts (BMA)
- Bachelor of Music Education (BME)
- Bachelor of Science in Music (BSM)

In the list above, the top four degrees are the ones most commonly earned by music majors, but you can see the variety of options. There are also post-secondary non-degree options. These include:

- Certificate
- Performance Diploma
- Undergraduate Diploma

Remember that non-degree programs provide training, but usually omit liberal arts classes. Since they are not degrees, it is not possible to enter a master's degree program after completing a non-degree undergraduate program.

While the list of degree programs is relatively short, the list of majors that we found is considerably longer. Schools add majors fairly often, usually in answer to a perceived need for training in a specific area. A few schools even have the option of creating your own major, which allows you to tailor your studies to your career goals. If you are looking for a program in an area that is less common, make sure you do your research. Here is a list of undergraduate music majors available within U.S. universities and colleges (keeping in mind that it is not definitive):

- Choral Music
- Commercial Music Production
- Composition
- Composition and Performance
- Contemporary Improvisation
- Contemporary Percussion and Mallet Keyboard
- Digital Arts and Sciences
- Ethnomusicology
- History and Literature
- Individualized Study in Musical Theatre
- Instrumental Music
- Jazz and Contemplative Studies
- Jazz and Contemporary Improvisation
- Jazz and Contemporary Music
- Jazz Performance – Instrumental
- Jazz Performance – Vocal
- Jazz Studies

- Medieval and Renaissance Studies
- Music
- Music and Sound Recording
- Music and Technology
- Music Business
- Music Business and Entertainment Industries
- Music Cognition
- Music Education
- Music Engineering
- Music History
- Music Industry
- Music Production
- Music Recording
- Music Studies
- Music Technology
- Music Theory
- Music Therapy
- Musical Theatre
- Musicology
- Performance
- Performance Jazz
- Performing Arts Technology
- Piano Performance and Vocal Accompaniment
- Popular Music
- Sacred Music
- Sound Engineering
- Technology and Applied Composition
- Technology and Related Arts

We found the following concentrations and emphases connected with BA and BFA degree programs:

- Choral/Vocal Music
- Early Music History Option
- General Music
- Instrumental Option
- Media Arts Concentration
- Music Concentration
- Music Education
- Music History Option
- Music Theory Option
- Piano
- Studio/Jazz Guitar
- Teacher Certification
- Vocal Option

Remember that degrees, majors, minors, concentrations, and emphases are based on math: the number of credit hours illustrates the weight of the focus. For example, a BME (Bachelor of Music Education) degree is likely to have more music education credits than a BM with a major in music education.

The following list illustrates some of the schools where you can find the different programs. This is NOT a definitive list. We urge you to do your own research to find the school and program that are the best match for your career goals. In other words, this list is presented to give you some idea of the breadth of options. (The list was drawn from the National Association of Schools of Music list of accredited institutions in 2017.)

Bachelor of Arts (in Music)

- American University (Washington DC)
- Ashland University (Ohio)
- Auburn University (Alabama)
- Augustana University (South Dakota)
- Belhaven University (Mississippi)
- Brevard College (North Carolina)
- California Polytechnic State University (California)
- California State University-Fullerton (California)
- California State University-San Bernardino (California)
- Cedarville University (Ohio)
- DePaul University (Illinois)
- Eastern Connecticut State University (Connecticut)
- Eastern Illinois University (Illinois)
- Emory University (Georgia)
- Evangel University (Missouri)
- George Washington University (Washington DC)
- Grand Canyon University (Arizona)
- Ithaca College (New York)
- Kentucky State University (Kentucky)
- Lebanon Valley College (Pennsylvania)
- Limestone College (South Carolina)
- Loyola University-New Orleans (Louisiana)
- Mansfield University (Pennsylvania)
- McNally Smith College of Music (Minnesota)
- Mercer University (Georgia)
- Mercyhurst University (Pennsylvania)
- Miami University (Ohio)
- Minnesota State University-Mankato (Minnesota)
- Missouri Southern State University (Missouri)
- Northwestern University (Illinois)
- Pennsylvania State University (Pennsylvania)

- Southwestern Baptist Theological Seminary (Texas)
- St. Ambrose University (Iowa)
- University of Central Florida (Florida)
- University of Georgia (Georgia)
- University of Maryland (Maryland)
- University of Miami (Florida)
- University of Missouri-Kansas City (Missouri)
- University of Nevada-Las Vegas (Nevada)
- University of North Carolina-Charlotte (North Carolina)
- University of North Carolina-Pembroke (North Carolina)
- University of the Pacific (California)
- University of South Carolina (South Carolina)
- University of Tampa (Florida)
- University of Texas-Austin (Texas)
- University of Vermont (Vermont)
- University of Wisconsin-Oshkosh (Wisconsin)
- Valparaiso University (Indiana)
- Wayland Baptist University (Texas)
- Wright State University (Ohio)
- Youngstown State University (Ohio)

Bachelor of Fine Arts (BFA)

- American Musical and Dramatic Academy (New York)
- Boston Conservatory at Berklee (Massachusetts)
- Carnegie Mellon University (Pennsylvania)
- Central Michigan University (Michigan)
- Florida State University (Florida)
- Sam Houston State University (Texas)
- University of Florida (Florida)
- University of Michigan (Michigan)
- Youngstown State University (Ohio)

Bachelor of Music (BM)

- Appalachian State University (North Carolina)
- Arizona State University (Arizona)
- Azusa Pacific University (California)
- Baldwin Wallace University (Ohio)
- Ball State University (Indiana)
- Baylor University (Texas)
- Berklee College of Music (Massachusetts)
- Boston Conservatory at Berklee (Massachusetts)
- Boston University (Massachusetts)
- Bowling Green State University (Ohio)
- Brigham Young University (Utah)
- Catholic University of America (Washington DC)
- Central Washington University (Washington)
- Chicago College of Performing Arts (Roosevelt University) (Illinois)
- Cleveland Institute of Music (Ohio)
- Cleveland State University (Ohio)
- Colburn School (California)
- Curtis Institute of Music (Pennsylvania)
- Delta State University (Mississippi)
- DePaul University (Illinois)
- Duquesne University (Pennsylvania)
- East Carolina University (North Carolina)
- Eastman School of Music (University of Rochester) (New York)
- Florida State University (Florida)
- Georgia State University (Georgia)
- Howard University (Washington DC)
- Indiana University (Indiana)
- Ithaca College (New York)
- Juilliard School (New York)
- Lawrence University (Wisconsin)

- Manhattan School of Music (New York)
- Mannes School of Music at the New School (New York)
- Metropolitan State University of Denver (Colorado)
- Michigan State University (Michigan)
- New England Conservatory (Massachusetts)
- Northern Arizona University (Arizona)
- Northwestern University (Illinois)
- Ohio State University (Ohio)
- Peabody Institute (Johns Hopkins University) (Maryland)
- Pennsylvania State University (Pennsylvania)
- San Francisco Conservatory of Music (California)
- Southern Methodist University (Texas)
- State University of New York-Potsdam (New York)
- Temple University (Pennsylvania)
- Texas Tech University (Texas)
- University of Cincinnati (Ohio)
- University of Colorado-Boulder (Colorado)
- University of Hartford (Connecticut)
- University of Houston (Texas)
- University of Louisville (Kentucky)
- University of Maryland (Maryland)
- University of Massachusetts-Amherst (Massachusetts)
- University of Miami (Florida)
- University of Michigan (Michigan)
- University of Missouri-Kansas City (Missouri)
- University of Nevada-Las Vegas (Nevada)
- University of North Carolina-Greensboro (North Carolina)
- University of Northern Colorado (Colorado)
- University of South Carolina (South Carolina)
- University of Tampa (Florida)
- University of Texas-Austin (Texas)
- University of Washington (Washington)

- Vanderbilt University (Tennessee)
- Westchester University of Pennsylvania (Pennsylvania)
- Wichita State University (Kansas)

Bachelor of Musical Arts (BMA)

- Bowling Green State University (Ohio)
- Pennsylvania State University (Pennsylvania)
- University of Michigan (Michigan)

Bachelor of Music Education (BME)

- Auburn University (Alabama)
- Baylor University (Texas)
- Chicago State University (Illinois)
- College of Wooster (Ohio)
- Drake University (Iowa)
- Emmanuel College (Georgia)
- Grand Valley State University (Michigan)
- Indiana University (Indiana)
- Loyola University-New Orleans (Louisiana)
- Mississippi State University (Mississippi)
- Montana State University (Montana)
- New Mexico State University (New Mexico)
- Pennsylvania State University (Pennsylvania)
- St. Ambrose University (Iowa)
- Texas Wesleyan University (Texas)
- University of Louisville (Kentucky)
- University of Maryland (Maryland)
- University of Nebraska-Lincoln (Nebraska)
- University of North Florida (Florida)
- University of Wisconsin-Oshkosh (Wisconsin)
- Valparaiso University (Indiana)

Bachelor of Science (BS)

- Adelphi University (New York)
- Appalachian State University (North Carolina)
- Augsburg College (Minnesota)
- Central Michigan University (Michigan)
- Duquesne University (Pennsylvania)
- Indiana University-Purdue University-Fort Wayne (Indiana)
- Indiana University-Purdue University-Indianapolis (Indiana)
- Kutztown University (Pennsylvania)
- Lebanon Valley College (Pennsylvania)
- Lipscomb University (Tennessee)
- Loyola University-New Orleans (Louisiana)
- Millersville University (Pennsylvania)
- Minnesota State University-Mankato (Minnesota)
- Minnesota State University-Moorhead (Minnesota)
- Saint Mary-of-the-Woods College (Indiana)
- Temple University (Pennsylvania)
- Towson University (Maryland)
- University of Evansville (Indiana)
- University of Indianapolis (Indiana)
- University of Missouri (Missouri)
- University of the Pacific (California)
- University of South Florida (Florida)
- University of Southern California (California)
- University of Wisconsin-Eau Claire (Wisconsin)
- University of Wisconsin-La Crosse (Wisconsin)
- University of Wisconsin-Oshkosh (Wisconsin)
- Western Connecticut State University (Connecticut)

Non-Degree Post-Secondary Programs

- Berklee College of Music (Massachusetts)
- Colburn School (California)

- Curtis Institute of Music (Pennsylvania)
- Juilliard School (New York)
- Longy School of Music of Bard College (Massachusetts)
- Mannes School of Music at the New School (New York)
- New England Conservatory (Massachusetts)
- Yale University (Connecticut)

To address the question of combined degree programs, here is a very short list of selected programs. Do your research to find others!

- Bard Conservatory and Bard College – BM and BA degrees (New York)

- Boston University College of Fine Arts and Boston University College of Arts and Science – BM and BA degrees (Massachusetts)

- Cleveland Institute of Music and Case Western Reserve University – BM and BA or BS (Ohio)

- Peabody Conservatory of Johns Hopkins University and Johns Hopkins University School of Arts and Sciences – BM and BA (Maryland)

- Lawrence University Conservatory of Music and Lawrence University – BM and BA (Wisconsin)

- New England Conservatory and Tufts University – BM and BA or BS (Massachusetts)

- Northwestern University Bienen School of Music and Northwestern University Weinberg College of Arts and Sciences – BM and BA (Illinois)

- Oberlin Conservatory and Oberlin College – BM and BA (Ohio)

- St. Olaf College Department of Music and St. Olaf College – BM and BA (Minnesota)

- University of Michigan School of Music, Theatre and Dance and University of Michigan Ross School of Business – BBA (Bachelor of Business and Arts) (Michigan)

- University of Redlands School of Music and University of Redland College of Arts and Sciences – BM and BA or BS (California)

- University of Rochester Eastman School of Music and University of Rochester College – BM and BA (New York)

APPENDIX 4
Application Materials Organizer

Create your own application materials organizer using this chart as a template. Add columns for each school to which you are applying, as needed, as well as adding rows for any additional requirements. See Chapter 5 for more guidance on using this chart.

	School #1	
GENERAL INFORMATION		
School Name		
School Location		
School Website		
Campus Visit		
Music Major Application Matrix (Tier 1, 2, 3, or 4) - see Chapter 4		
Tuition Cost (published amount)		
Room & Board Cost (published amount)		
APPLICATION ITEMS		
Application Due Date		
Application Fee Amount		
Transcript Ordered (to be sent directly from the issuing school)		
Test Scores Submitted: SAT, ACT, Subject Tests, TOEFL, etc. (if required)		
Essay #1 Written & Submitted		
Essay #2 Written & Submitted (if required)		
Recommendation #1 Requested		
Rec #1 Thank You Sent to Recommender		
Recommendation #2 Requested		
Rec #2 Thank You Sent to Recommender		
Recommendation #3 Requested		
Rec #3 Thank You Sent to Recommender		
Portfolio/Supplemental Materials Submitted (if required)		
FINANCIAL AID MATERIALS		
FAFSA Submitted (available online after October 1)		
CSS Profile Submitted (if required)		
Application(s) for school-specific scholarships (find on school's website)		
PRESCREENING RECORDING REQUIREMENTS		
Prescreening Recording Required		
AUDITION PLANNING		
Audition Date Preference #1 (date, location)		
Audition Date Preference #2 (date, location)		
Audition Date Preference #3 (date, location)		
FINAL AUDITION SCHEDULE		
Audition Date		
Audition Location		
Travel Arrangements Made (transportation, accommodations, etc.)		

	School #2	School #3	School #4	School #5	School #6	School #7

APPENDIX 5
Sample Application Fee Waiver Request

Search on a school's website for an application fee waiver form or protocol. If you cannot find this information, contact the music school's admissions office. Be honest about your situation, and provide enough detail for the admissions office to make an informed decision.

SAMPLE EMAIL REQUESTING AN APPLICATION FEE WAIVER

To Whom It May Concern:

My name is [your name], and I am a [name of instrument: vocalist, trumpet player, etc.] completing my senior year at [name of high school]. I am extremely interested in attending [name of institution] for my [name of specific degree school offers] in the fall of [year you would be entering school]. I am not able to pay the [$ amount] application fee required to apply. [Explain why; for example: I am currently working part time and fully supporting myself financially without help from family to aid in my schooling.] If you offer application fee waivers, please let me know how I may request one.

Thank you for your time.

Sincerely,
[your name]
[your email]
[your cell phone number]

APPENDIX 6

The College Essay/Personal Statement: Purpose and Prompts

Most college applications require a writing sample in one form or another. There are two main reasons for this:

- To see if the applicant can write competently

- To get a feel for the applicant's personality, clarity of thought, use of language

The first reason—to see if the applicant can write competently—is basic: Do you use correct spelling, grammar, and punctuation?

The second reason—to get a feel for the applicant—means that you have an opportunity to express yourself in writing, and let the admissions committee get to know you a little bit. Just remember this: Every single thing you do, write, or submit as part of your application is assessed. If you scribble an essay thirty minutes before the application deadline, odds are that it will not be your best work. That is not a good thing, because other applicants will have taken more time to truly represent themselves. Do not have someone else write the essay for you: it will not serve you as a candidate and it can often be detected, which is grounds for immediate rejection.

If you are not a native English speaker and you have someone translate your essay from your native language into flawless English, that, too, can be detected.

To help you start thinking in the right direction, we have assembled a few sample essay/personal statement prompts. As noted previously in the book, as soon as an application is available you can start writing your essay, even if it's the summer before senior year. Most of the prompts are broad enough that you do not have to wait until the deadline to write a good essay.

Common Application Essay Prompts (as of August 2018)

The Common Application is used by many music schools, including Bard, Carnegie Mellon, Northwestern, Oberlin, University of Miami, Yale, and others. Essay length is capped at 650 words.

- Some students have a background, identity, interest, or talent that is so meaningful they believe their application would be incomplete without it. If this sounds like you, then please share your story.

- The lessons we take from obstacles we encounter can be fundamental to later success. Recount a time when you faced a challenge, setback, or failure. How did it affect you, and what did you learn from the experience?

- Reflect on a time when you questioned or challenged a belief or idea. What prompted your thinking? What was the outcome?

- Describe a problem you've solved or a problem you'd like to solve. It can be an intellectual challenge, a research query, an ethical dilemma—anything that is of personal importance, no matter the scale. Explain its significance to you and what steps you took or could be taken to identify a solution.

- Discuss an accomplishment, event, or realization that sparked a period of personal growth and a new understanding of yourself or others.

- Describe a topic, idea, or concept you find so engaging that it makes you lose all track of time. Why does it captivate you? To what or to whom do you turn to when you want to learn more?

- Share an essay on any topic of your choice. It can be one you've already written, one that responds to a different prompt, or one of your own design.

San Francisco Conservatory of Music's Essay (as of August 2018)

Applicants must submit responses to the following writing prompts:

- Please describe the factors that will guide your collegiate admission decision and briefly discuss why, specifically, you have applied to SFCM. (300-500 words)

- Please include a brief essay discussing your career goals as a professional musician. (300-500 words)

The Juilliard School's Essay Requirements and Topics (as of August 2018)

Juilliard's Admissions Committee uses your essay(s) to learn more about you as an individual and gain a sense of who you are beyond your application, transcript, and audition.

Essay Requirements
- 1–2 pages, double-spaced, 12-point font
- written in English (not translated from another language)
- must be your own original work
- submitted within the online application

Choose one of the following topics:
- Many artists experience a moment that crystallizes their career goals. Describe what that moment was for you. Be specific and tell us how that moment continues to influence your artistic and academic work to this day.
- The Cambridge Dictionary defines integrity as "the quality of being honest and having strong moral principles," as well as "wholeness and unity." How would you define artistic integrity for yourself and your art form?

Optional Essay
- Should you have a special personal or academic history that you feel can explain an unusual circumstance—a gap year, unusually low or poor grades in a semester or year, etc.—you have the option to submit an additional short essay.

The Juilliard School also requires additional essays if you are applying as a transfer student.

WRITING HELP

If you need help with your essay, there are companies and professionals that specialize in helping high school students organize, write, and proofread essays. This assistance can be costly but a great help to certain students. (Note that these are companies that *help* students— these are not companies that *write* essays for the students. That is considered unethical.) If you are looking for a less expensive option, try the book *College Essay Guide* by Ethan Sawyer.

APPENDIX 7
Sample Résumé

Schools request résumés in order to have a quick way to view information about the applicant. Your task is to do this in a one-page document, using an outline format or bullet points to briefly provide the information. We have provided a sample résumé on the next page. It is not necessary to follow this sample exactly, but you should include these elements.

Cathleen Anne Green, Violin
123 Street Address
City, State 90089
yourname@gmail.com   123.123.1234

EDUCATION	Los Angeles High School, Los Angeles, CA	
	2014-2018	
	GPA: 3.72	
TEACHERS	Niccolò Paganini	2016-2018
	Dorothy DeLay	Summer 2014
	Leopold Auer	2012-2016
ENSEMBLE	Local Youth Orchestra, concertmaster	2015-2017
EXPERIENCE	Illinois Summer Arts Festival Orchestra	Summer 2014
	Los Angeles High School String Quartet	2015-2018
HONORS &	From the Top	April 2018
AWARDS	Concerto Winner, Local Youth Orchestra	May 2017
	California ASTA First Prize	January 2016
	LA High School, Tennis Captain	2016-2017
	Creative Writing Prize, LAUSD	Fall 2016
OTHER	Trader Joe's, stockroom clerk	Summer 2016
EXPERIENCE	Nursing Home, holiday recital	December 2017

REMINDERS:

- Résumés are NOT program bios. They are requested instead of bios because the list format makes it easy for faculty and admissions committees to scan quickly.

- You may include other information on your résumé, but keep it short. Do not send copies of programs from your concerts and recitals unless specifically asked to send them.

APPENDIX 8
Sample Repertoire Lists

Sometimes schools require you to submit a repertoire list; this is a list of musical works you have studied. If a rep list is not required, do not submit it. If it is required, be aware of the following points:

- List your name, your instrument, and the degree to which you are applying at the top of your repertoire list.

- Limit your list to repertoire learned in the last four years unless you have covered a significant amount of standard repertoire early in your career, or unless you are asked for a more specific period.

- List the composer, the name of the work(s), and whether or not you performed it. Sometimes the date of performance is required (month and year are usually sufficient).

- Programs from concerts or recitals should not be included with your repertoire list unless requested in the application requirements.

SAMPLE STRING REPERTOIRE LIST

In each section, include only works studied in the last four years; list them alphabetically by composer's last name.

Your Name, BM Applicant, Violin Performance
Repertoire List *(August 2014-2018)*

Concertos

- Composer, Concerto Name, movement(s) studied, if and when performed

Sonatas

- Composer, Sonata Name, movement(s) studied, if and when performed

Etudes/Caprices

- Composer, Name of Work

Chamber Music

- Composer, Name of Work, movement(s) studied, if and when performed

Orchestral Works

- List only if you had a substantial solo (for example, *Scheherazade* or *Don Quixote*)

SAMPLE WINDS, BRASS, PERCUSSION, AND HARP REPERTOIRE LIST

In each section, include only works studied in the last four years; list them alphabetically by composer's last name.

Your Name, BM Applicant, Flute Performance
Repertoire List *(August 2014-2018)*

Solos
- Composer, Name of Work, movement(s) studied, if and when performed

Orchestral Works Performed
- Composer, Name of Work

Orchestral Excerpts Learned
- Composer, Name of Work

Etudes
- Composer, Name of Work/Book

Chamber Music
- Composer, Name of Work, movement(s) studied, if and when performed

SAMPLE PIANO REPERTOIRE LIST

In each section, include only works studied in the last four years; list them alphabetically by composer's last name.

Your Name, BM Applicant, Piano Performance
Repertoire List *(August 2014-2018)*

Sonatas

- Composer, Sonata Name, movement(s) studied, if and when performed

Concertos

- Composer, Concerto Name, movement(s) studied, if and when performed

Virtuoso Works

- Composer, Name of Work, movement(s) studied, if and when performed

Chamber Music

- Composer, Name of Work, movement(s) studied, if and when performed

SAMPLE VOICE REPERTOIRE LIST

In each section, include only works studied in the last four years; list them alphabetically by composer's last name.

Your Name, BM Applicant, Voice Performance
Repertoire List *(August 2014-2018)*

Art Songs
- Composer, Song Title, if and when performed

Arias
- Composer, Name of Work, if and when performed

Opera Productions and/or Musical Theatre Works Performed
- Composer, Name of Work, if and when performed

APPENDIX 9
Prescreening Recording: A How-To for Applicants

Applicants wishing to record a supplemental tape for a non-music major application can follow the same guidelines listed here for prescreening recordings.

THE "WHAT" AND "WHY" OF PRESCREENING

"Prescreening" is the process used by music schools to manage their applicant pools, usually in vocal and instrumental performance majors. It can also be used for non-performance majors such as composition. Prescreening is typically required in areas with large numbers of applicants (such as violin, flute, piano, or soprano), but some schools prescreen all instruments and voices as a matter of policy. When a prescreening recording is required, it acts as a first audition round; applicants may be denied admission based on the prescreening round without ever auditioning in person. While that may seem harsh, there are several advantages:

- If you are invited, you will have a less-crowded audition day to navigate, which benefits both you and the faculty.

- You will save the time and cost of travel if not invited to a live audition.

- You can focus on the other schools to which you have applied if you are not invited to a live audition.

- You will really polish and perfect repertoire during the pre-screening recording process, which will benefit you when performing the same repertoire at your live auditions.

COSTS

Costs involved in making recordings can include:

- HD camera/microphone or recording team

- Hall/room use (rental fee)

- A pianist, if accompaniment is required for the recording

- Cost of the teacher's time to attend the recording session (if applicable)

Most schools do not expect you to make a professional-quality recording, nor do schools want you to invest hundreds of dollars in this process. What really matters to a school is that the recording represents your playing. A poor-quality recording can ruin your chances of being invited to audition. The best way to prevent this is to plan ahead and avoid rushing through this process.

LOCATION & DRESS

You will first need a location. Since you want to present yourself in the most favorable way, it makes sense to find a place where you will sound your best. The room should not be too dry, or too live. Prescreening recordings can be made in recital halls, teachers' studios, applicants' living rooms, churches, etc. A practice room is rarely the best place to record an audition.

You will likely have several selections to record, and you may want to do this over several days to avoid fatigue. Whatever space you use, reserve the same room/hall and present yourself in the same manner (same hairstyle, clothes, etc.) for each day of recording. This way the videos appear continuous. You do not typically have to record everything in one take without breaks, but having consistency keeps it simple. Also, dress nicely for the video recordings. If you have never met the professor(s) that will be watching the video, this will be the very first impression they have of you. (Obviously, if the recording is audio, then concerns about dress do not apply.)

EQUIPMENT

The majority of conservatories and universities require video rather than audio recordings. This allows a teacher to meet you, hear you, and see your technique. Most schools will request that each piece appear on a separate track; however, no editing (audio or video, including the addition of reverb) should take place within an individual track. Although some students hire a professional recording team, this is not necessary or required. It is preferable, though, to have someone in the hall (ideally your teacher) to hit start and stop on the camera, set the levels, take notes about tracks that need to be redone, and give feedback when necessary.

Among musicians, the most popular high definition (HD) camera with a great microphone is made by the company ZOOM (Q4, Q8, etc.): https://www.zoom.co.jp/. Try to purchase the model that has a microphone with changeable gain control (1-10). The cameras usually cost about $300, but are worth the investment since many students will use them again to make summer festival audition recordings, YouTube videos, and even to record lessons, masterclasses, and practice sessions.

CAMERA PLACEMENT AND LEVELS

When recording, make sure the camera is placed in such a way that the faculty can see your technique (i.e., do not put a music stand in front of a string player's bow arm or zoom out far so that it is impossible to see a wind player's mouth). Also check that the levels on the sound input are adjusted so that the microphone is not clipping.

ACCOMPANIST

If an accompanist is required for the prescreening recordings, make sure to book the accompanist at least two weeks in advance, and plan a rehearsal prior to the recording. Try to rehearse in the same space in which you will record. At the very least, make sure the accompanist has tried out the piano ahead of time to make sure it is adequate and tuned. The best preparation for a recording is performing the solo repertoire in a recital (especially if it is in the same space and with the same accompanist).

REPERTOIRE

Use the instructions in Chapter 6 to help make your repertoire binder, so that all of your prescreening repertoire is organized and in one place. You will be relieved to see that there is some overlap within the repertoire (the same work is on multiple lists) or that the requirements are broad enough that you can use the same work for more than one school.

SCHEDULING

Because prescreening determines if you are invited to a live audition, making the prescreening recording is often the most stressful part of the entire audition process. Take it seriously, and allow enough time to complete all the steps required—not just the playing part, but also the organizing, getting the space, rehearsing with the accompanist, and uploading the final product.

When scheduling the number of hours of prescreening recording, plan for about 20-30 minutes per orchestral excerpt or piece and about one hour per solo, aria, or étude. The amount of time varies per student and per amount of repertoire to be recorded. However, the average amount of prescreening recording hours usually translates into approximately 8-10 hours per student.

Once you know what repertoire you need to record, make a tentative schedule of what you want to record each day, and in what order. For example, you may want to record more challenging works earlier in the day, when you are less tired. Recording sessions should always be broken down into two- or three-hour blocks, with breaks every 30-45 minutes. For players who experience physical fatigue (brass players and singers, for example), you may find that shorter recording sessions (two hours or less) work better. Most students will schedule these sessions to take place over several days with a day or two off in between.

It is normal for some days to go better than others. In the schedule, allow for at least one to two days of recording to be "cleanup days," when repertoire can be rerecorded if needed. Depending on the success of previous sessions, you may or may not even need these days.

DEADLINES

Allow ample time to find your favorite takes and upload your material (estimate at least another five hours). The time needed post-recording to gather these takes and upload material is often underestimated and can add a great deal of unwanted stress, so plan ahead.

Note the deadline for the recording submission. Is this a "postmark deadline" or a "received by" deadline? If it is to be uploaded online, note that *every other applicant to that school has the same deadline*. When everyone waits until the last minute, this can create problems with the technology, such as slow upload times or frozen portals. In order to make the school's deadline, set your own deadline for uploading at least one week prior. Some schools will not process your application until the recording has been received. If the recording is late, then your application may be considered late, too.

POSITIVE SIDE OF PRESCREENING

On the positive side, making the recordings is great practice for the live audition, affording multiple opportunities to play the repertoire under pressure. In the end, you may find that you enjoy recording more than auditioning live. However, it is recommended to apply to two or three schools that do not require prescreening. Knowing that there is a chance to audition live no matter what will take some of the pressure off you.

APPENDIX 10
Audition Repertoire List Examples

Appendices 10 and 12 are meant to work together to manage repertoire lists. An added bonus is that by completing Appendices 10 and 12
sequentially, you can reduce repertoire stress.

To start, print a copy of the repertoire that each school is requiring, and
put it in your Repertoire Binder so that all of the information lives in
one place. We have provided here examples of tenor trombone repertoire lists for seven schools. Your job is to print out each list and add it
to your Repertoire Binder. Then proceed to Appendix 12.

(Note: These schools are chosen for illustration, and do not constitute
a recommendation or endorsement. The repertoire lists included have
been copied directly from each school's website. If you are following
the advice in this book, you will create a list of schools that uniquely fits
your individual goals.)

Bob Cole Conservatory of Music at California State University, Long Beach
Undergraduate Tenor Trombone Repertoire (as of August 2018)

An audition is required for admittance to all degree programs in the Bob Cole Conservatory of Music. Conservatory admission auditions take place in October (for Spring admission) and February (for Fall admission). If there are circumstances that prevent your attendance at the scheduled auditions, you may contact the Area Director to arrange an individual appointment.

Audition Requirements
Applicants for admission should be prepared to perform: One or more selections from the standard repertoire that reflect both lyrical and technical proficiency. Auditions will take place before the Area Director and appropriate faculty members of the Bob Cole Conservatory of Music.

Colburn School Conservatory of Music
Undergraduate Tenor Trombone Repertoire (as of August 2018)

Prescreening Recording Required

Prescreening Repertoire
The first step of the audition process is for you, the applicant, to upload a prescreening video recording by the December 1st application deadline. Piano accompaniment is preferred, but not required, for prescreening. The prescreening video recording must contain the following repertoire:

1. One etude from Bordogni Melodious Etudes, Book One (Rochut)

2. Two contrasting movements from a solo of the applicant's choice

3. Orchestral excerpts:

   - Mozart Tuba Mirum from the Requiem

   - Rossini Overture to La Gazza Ladra (from the Keith Brown orchestral excerpts books) – All 3 excerpts

   - Wagner Tannhauser Overture – the ¾ section

Live Audition Repertoire
- If you are invited to audition, you must prepare works from each category listed below. Piano accompaniment is required. A list of pianists will be provided.

Scales
- All major and minor scales, two octaves, both slurred and tongued

Etudes
- Blazhevich Clef Studies (bass, tenor and alto clefs) – Etudes #67 and #71

Solo Work
- One slow and one fast movement from a concerto of the applicant's choice

OR

- Choose one of the following:
  ○ Guilman Morceau Symphonique
  ○ Lars Erik Larsson Concertino
  ○ Serocki Sonatine

Orchestral Excerpts
- Berlioz Hungarian March
- Mozart Tuba Mirum from the Requiem
- Ravel Bolero
- Rossini Overture to La Gazza Ladra (all sections)
- Wagner Ride of the Valkyries (major and minor sections)

The Juilliard School
Undergraduate Tenor Trombone Repertoire (as of August 2018)

Prescreening Recording Required

Prescreening and Live Audition Repertoire
1. B-flat, C, and D Major and minor (harmonic) scales, played in two octaves (detached), starting from low B-flat, C, and D, all in the staff in bass clef.
2. Two etudes showing the applicant's level of technical and musical advancement.
3. At least one major solo of the applicant's choice.
4. The following orchestral excerpts:
   - MOZART: Requiem, K. 626 ("Tuba mirum")
   - ROSSINI: La Gazza Ladra
   - RAVEL: Bolero
   - MAHLER 3: 3 measures after #13 to #17

Northwestern University Bienen School of Music
Undergraduate Tenor Trombone Repertoire (as of August 2018)

*Prescreening Recording Required

Prescreening required; must be video recording. Video should be shot from left side so mouthpiece is clearly visible.

For Prescreening and Final Audition:

All repertoire required. No substitutions.

Solo Selection:
- Saint-Saëns, Cavatine Op.144

Orchestral Excerpts:
- Berlioz, Hungarian March (second trombone)
- Mozart, Requiem "Tuba Mirum" (second trombone)
- Ravel, Bolero
- Saint-Saëns, Symphony No. 3 in C Minor, slow movement
- Wagner, Die Walküre "Ride of the Valkyries," B Maj. section

Shepherd School of Music Rice University
Undergraduate Tenor Trombone Repertoire (as of August 2018)

*Prescreening Recording Required

Preliminary submission is by video
- Two contrasting movements from a Baroque sonata
- Solo of your choice
- Orchestral Excerpts:

- · Mozart Tuba Mirum from Requiem
- · Ravel Trombone Solo from Bolero
- · Berlioz Hungarian March (2nd trombone part)
- · Schumann Symphony No. 3, "Rhenisch" 4th mvt.
  (1st trombone part)
- · Mahler Symphony No. 3, trombone solos from 1st mvt.
- · Wagner Ride of the Valkyries

Required Tenor Trombone Live Audition Repertoire
- • One Sonata by a Baroque composer such as Galliard, Marcello, Handel, Vivaldi, Telemann, or Corelli
- • One of the following: Dutilleux Chorale, Cadence et Fugato; Grondahl Concerto; Larsson Concertino, or Solo of your choice of comparable difficulty
- • Orchestral Excerpts:
  - · Mozart Tuba Mirum from Requiem
  - · Ravel Trombone Solo from Bolero
  - · Berlioz Hungarian March (2nd trombone part)
  - · Schumann Symphony No. 3, "Rhenisch" 4th mvt.
    (1st trombone part)
  - · Mahler Symphony No. 3, trombone solos from 1st mvt.
  - · Wagner Ride of the Valkyries
- • Major Scales two octaves
- • Sight reading (may include Tenor and Alto Clefs)

San Francisco Conservatory
Undergraduate Tenor Trombone Repertoire (as of August 2018)

Undergraduate (repertoire does not need to be memorized)
1. Études from J. Rochut Melodious Études, Book 1
2. Solo of choice with contrasting sections
3. Excerpts from the symphonic repertoire (Ravel Bolero, Mozart Requiem: Tuba mirum, Berlioz Hungarian March). (Incoming freshmen excluded).
4. Sight reading

University of Southern California Thornton School of Music
Undergraduate Tenor Trombone Repertoire (as of August 2018)

*Prescreening Recording Required

Piano accompaniment is NOT required. Audio or video recordings are acceptable for prescreen. Audition repertoire for all degree levels is the same for the live audition and prescreen recording.

Tenor Trombone:
- A movement from each of two solo pieces of contrasting styles.
- Orchestral excerpts from:
  - Trombone solo from the Mozart Requiem
  - Wagner- Ride of the Walküre
  - Rossini- La Gazza Ladra
  - Ravel- Bolero

APPENDIX 11
Audition Information for Repertoire Binder

This page provides you with a quick overview of critical audition information. It goes together with Appendices 10 and 12 to help you organize your audition preparations. Include this chart in your Repertoire Binder.

	School #1	
AUDITION PLANNING		
Prescreening Recording Required?		
Audition Date		
Audition Location		

	School #2	School #3	School #4	School #5	School #6	School #7

APPENDIX 12
Master List of Audition Repertoire

Before creating this Master List of Audition Repertoire, make sure you follow the instructions in Appendix 10.

Once you have decided where to apply, combine the repertoire lists from each separate school into one Master List. This allows you to see where the lists overlap. Rather than learning the material for each individual school, approach the repertoire as one large list. This may sound overwhelming, but you will find that learning the repertoire actually becomes more manageable. For example, some audition lists have very specific repertoire requirements, while other lists have more generalized requirements. (For comparison, look at Appendix 10 and compare Cal State Long Beach's list with the Colburn School's list.) The strategy is to minimize the number of works to learn by reusing the specific works required by some schools for those schools whose requirements are not specific.

It is important to make note of which pieces are needed for pre-screening and which ones are needed for the live auditions. For some instruments, prescreening pieces will differ from those required for live auditions. In the sample Master List, the pieces marked with (*) are required for both prescreening and live auditions.

Taking the tenor trombone lists from Appendix 10 and merging them together, one can see that all those lists reduce down to this:

Tenor Trombone Master List of Prescreening and Live Audition Repertoire (August of 2018)

- Scales & Arpeggios
    - B-flat, C, and D Major and minor (harmonic) scales, played in two octaves (detached), starting from low B-flat, C, and D, all in the staff in bass clef*
    - All major and minor scales, two octaves, both slurred and tongued
- Solos
    - Saint-Saëns, *Cavatine*, Op. 144*
    - David, Concerto for Trombone. First page through the low Bb at the bottom of the page (no cadenza)*
    - Two contrasting movements from a solo of the applicant's choice OR one of the following: Guilmant *Morceau Symphonique,* Lars-Erik Larsson *Concertino,* Dutilleux *Chorale, Cadence et Fugato,* Grondahl *Concerto,* or Serocki *Sonatine**
    - Two contrasting movements from a Baroque sonata by a composer such as Galliard, Marcello, Handel, Vivaldi, Telemann, or Corelli*
- Excerpts
    - Berlioz, *Hungarian March* (2nd trombone)*
    - Mahler, Symphony No. 3, measures after #13 to #17 and all trombone solos from movement 1*
    - Mozart, *Requiem*, K. 626 "Tuba Mirum" (2nd trombone)*

- Ravel, *Bolero**

- Rossini, *La Gazza Ladra (Keith Brown orchestral excerpts book - 3 excerpts)**

- Saint-Saëns, Symphony No. 3 in C minor, slow movement*

- Schumann, Symphony No. 3 "Rhenisch," movement 4 (1st trombone part)*

- Wagner, *Die Walkure* "Ride of the Valkyries", major and minor section*

- Wagner, *Tannhauser Overture* (¾ section)*

- Études

  - Blazhevich *Clef Studies*, études #67 and #71 (bass, tenor, and alto clefs)

  - One étude of choice from Rochut *Melodius Études*, vol. 1

- Other

  - Sight reading (may include tenor and alto clef)

Looking over this master list, you can see that instead of having seven unique lists, you actually have one very manageable set of requirements.

APPENDIX 13
Sample Emails Declining an Offer of Admission

If you decide to decline an offer of admission, you are obligated to inform the school's designated admissions officer—not the applied teacher—of your decision. If you notify the school through an appplication portal, there may be no need for an email to the admissions office, but it is a professional courtesy to notify the applied teacher as well. Samples of both types of emails are given here.

SAMPLE EMAIL TO THE ADMISSIONS OFFICE

To Whom It May Concern:

I would like to thank you for the offer of admission to the [name of school]. This decision has not been an easy one, and while I absolutely admire both the faculty and institution, I have decided to attend [name of institution that you will be attending]. Thank you for your time and understanding.

Sincerely,

[your name]

[your email]

[your cell phone number]

It is also recommended to send a message to the applied professor.

SAMPLE EMAIL TO THE APPLIED TEACHER

Dear Professor (last name of applied instructor),

I am writing to let you know how grateful I am for the offer of admission to the [name of school]. This decision has not been an easy one, and while I absolutely admire you, your studio, and the institution, I have decided to attend [name of institution that you will be attending]. I hope to have the opportunity to work with you again in the future. Thank you for your time and understanding.

Sincerely,
[your name]
[your email]
[your cell phone number]

APPENDIX 14
Sample Waitlist Status Emails

ON THE WAITLIST

Many schools do not communicate much information to a student who is placed on a waitlist. As mentioned in Chapter 9, the National Association for College Admissions Counseling (https://www.nac-acnet.org/) provides information and advice on waitlists. If you have been placed on a waitlist, here are some questions that you should ask the institution that has waitlisted you:

1. Is the school's waitlist ranked or unranked? (A ranked waitlist means the students are listed on a waitlist in the order the school would accept them.)

2. If ranked, where do I fall on the waitlist?

3. What is the average percentage of students accepted from the waitlist on my instrument? (In the music world, this percentage can vary greatly by instrument. For example, a school may admit students each year from the violin waitlist, but only occasionally from the flute waitlist.)

If you are placed on a waitlist, it is your responsibility to communicate with the school to stay on that list. The school will need the following information from you:

1.   Whether or not you wish to be kept on the waitlist

2.   If the school is your first choice

Note that music schools tend to have relatively small waitlists because the waitlists are maintained according to majors (for example, five flute applicants on the flute waitlist, fifteen violin applicants on the violin waitlist, etc). Non-music colleges and universities tend to have larger waitlists. One college had over 1,000 applicants on the waitlist. That is a very different situation than being one of ten on a waitlist!

SAMPLE EMAIL TO ASK WHERE YOU ARE ON THE WAITLIST

Assuming that you received very little information from the school (that is, that you only know that you have been placed on the waitlist), here is a sample email that should be sent prior to May 1:

To Whom It May Concern:

I received a notice stating that I am on the [instrument] waitlist for this coming fall. In order to make the best decision, can you let me know where I rank on the waitlist? Also, how many [instrumentalists, i.e., violinists, trumpet players, singers, etc.] do you typically admit from the waitlist each year? Since it is before May 1, can you say if it appears likely that you will take anyone off the waitlist before that date?

As you know, I need to make a commitment to a school by May 1. [Name of this school] is definitely my first choice. Please keep me on the waitlist, and let me know as soon as possible if my status changes. Thank you in advance for your time.

Sincerely,
[your name]
[your email]
[your cell phone number]

OFF THE WAITLIST

If you are taken off the waitlist and given a spot at an institution after May 1, make sure to weigh all of your options before you accept the school's offer. Wait until you receive your acceptance in writing. Are you happy with the financial aid package? If not, review Chapter 10 and Appendix 15, "Making an Appeal." If you decide to stay at the institution where you have already enrolled, simply decline the new offer of admission. If you decide that you wish to commit to this new institution, you will need to:

1. Write an email to the school where you enrolled. Ask to be released from that institution because you have been taken off the waitlist and accepted to your first-choice school.

2. Write an email to the professor at the school where you enrolled. Tell them you have been accepted to your first-choice institution and that you will be enrolling there instead.

3. Write to the professor at the school where you were accepted off the waitlist, and tell them that you will be enrolling.

SAMPLE EMAIL TO THE ADMISSIONS OFFICE
OF THE SCHOOL WHERE YOU INITIALLY ENROLLED

To Whom It May Concern:

I received an offer of admission from [school that accepted you off the waitlist] stating that I have been accepted off the waitlist. While this has been a difficult decision for me and I was excited to attend your institution in the fall, I have decided to cancel my enrollment here and enroll at [school that accepted you off the waitlist]. I understand that my enrollment deposit is non-refundable.

Please let me know if you need anything further from me. Thank you for your consideration.

Sincerely,
[your name]
[your email]
[your cell phone number]

.

SAMPLE EMAIL TO THE APPLIED PROFESSOR
OF THE SCHOOL WHERE YOU INITIALLY ENROLLED

Dear Professor [last name of applied instructor],

I received a notice from [school that accepted you off the waitlist] stating that I have been accepted off the waitlist. After much thought, I have decided to cancel my enrollment at [enrolled school] and enroll at [school that accepted you off the waitlist]. I am very grateful for the possibility of studying with you, and I hope to be able to work with you at some point in the future.

Thank you for your understanding.

Sincerely,
[your name]
[your email]
[your cell phone number]

FINAL NOTE

Remember that all official communication must be with the admissions office, not just the professor, for anything related to the status of your application.

APPENDIX 15
Sample Email Appealing Financial Aid Package

Some institutions allow admitted students to appeal for an increase in their aid package. Other institutions will consider an appeal only in extraordinary circumstances. If the school is your first-choice school and it is not affordable with the aid offered, you and your family may consider appealing for more funding. The period between notice of admission (usually around April 1) and the response deadline of May 1 is the time for applicants to consider the aid package. Do this as soon as possible, since schools do not have unlimited budgets and it is possible that at some point they will be unable to offer more aid.

Note that schools consider appeals because they want you to be able to enroll. They do not consider appeals because an applicant is playing one school off of another. The best assumption for all involved is that you are sincere in your desire to attend the school to which you are appealing.

SAMPLE EMAIL OF APPEAL TO THE APPROPRIATE OFFICE

This email is usually sent to either the Financial Aid Office or the Music Admissions Office.

To Whom It May Concern:

I was very excited to be accepted into [name of school] and Professor [last name of applied instructor]'s studio. Thank you for the initial scholarship offer of $[list amount of aid awarded].

After visiting the campus for my audition, taking a lesson with Professor [last name of applied instructor], and learning more about the program, it became clear to me that [name of school] is my number one choice school. [Explain your situation, i.e., I am the youngest of three children, my older siblings are in college, my family lives off a single income, etc.]

After speaking with my parents about the finances, I would need an additional $[name the amount needed] to attend. Is there someone with whom I should speak about my need? I appreciate any advice that you can give. I truly hope to attend [name of school] in the fall.

Thank you for your time.

Sincerely,
[your name]
[your email]
[your cell phone number]

APPENDIX 16
The Music Industry: Careers in Music

The careers listed in this appendix are chosen to illustrate the many paths available in the music industry. This list is not exhaustive; undoubtedly new careers will be invented in the future. See the "Careers in Music" section on www.collegeprepformusicians.com for more information.

Arts Administration

- Artist Relations
- Audition Coordinator
- Development
- Education
- Financing
- Grant Writing
- Human Resources
- Major Gifts/Fundraising
- Marketing
- Music Director
- Orchestra Manager
- President/CEO
- Public Relations
- Stage Hand/Tech Crew

Composer/Songwriter

Conductor/Music Director

- Broadway Shows
- Choir
- Church/Choral
- Contemporary
- Film, TV, and Video Games
- Opera
- Pop Music
- Symphony Orchestra

Film Music, TV, and Video Games

- Composer
- Conductor
- Contractor
- Copyist
- Engineer
- Licensing Representative
- Mixer
- Music Editor
- Musician
- Music Supervisor
- Orchestrator
- Producer
- Songwriter
- Stage Manager/Stage Hand
- Studio Music Executive

Instrument Maker and Repairer

Management

- Agent (representing composers, ensembles, pop artists, soloists, etc.)
- Artist
- Contracts
- Labels
- Recording

Music and Medicine

- Acupuncturist
- Alexander Technique Instructor
- Applied Kinesiologist
- Body Mapping Specialist
- Feldenkrais Practitioner
- Gerontology Specialist
- Massage Therapist
- Music and the Brain Researcher
- Music Therapist (for Children, the Elderly, Musicians)
- Performance Psychologist
- Physical Therapist
- Psychologist
- Researcher

Music Critic/Journalist
- Book, Blog, Magazine, and Journal Writer
- Concert Reviewer
- Researcher

Music Education
- Band/Choir/Orchestra Director
- Classroom Teacher (music history, music theory, solfège, etc.)
- College Professor
- Early Childhood Educator
- Kodaly, Orff, Suzuki, and Dalcroze Certified Instructor
- Lecturer
- Music in Schools Specialist (National Education Standards)
- Pre-College Classroom Teacher (elementary, middle school, secondary levels)
- Private Studio Teacher

Music Entrepreneur
- Business Owner
- Social Media "Influencer"

Music Law
- Contracts
- Lawyer (entertainment law)
- Licensing
- Politician

Music Librarian
- Film
- Opera
- Orchestra
- School/Academia

Music Ministry
- Cantor
- Choir Director
- Organist
- Praise Band
- Singer/Choir Member

Music Preparation

- Arranger
- Copyist
- Orchestrator

Music Video Production

- Choreographer
- Cinematographer
- Conductor
- Contractor
- Director
- Engineer
- Producer

Music Publishing/Record Labels

- Artists and Repertoire Scout (A&R)
- Catalog Development
- Licensing
- Marketing/Promotion/ Publicity

Music Retail

- Album Sales
- Instrument Repair
- Instrument Sales and Rental
- Marketing
- Music Sales
- Ticket Sales

Musician/Performer

- Broadway Show Pit Orchestra Musician
- Chamber Musician
- Choir Member
- Church/Choral Musician
- Collaborative Pianist (Ballet, Instrumental, Vocal)
- Commercial Musician
- Contemporary Musician
- Film, TV, and Video Game Music Recording Artist
- Jazz Musician
- Military Ensemble Musician
- Opera Singer
- Pop Musician
- Solo Artist
- Symphony Orchestra Musician

Physics and Music

- Acoustician/Architect
- Physics of Music Teacher
- Researcher

Piano Technician

- Tuner
- Builder
- Repairer

Radio/TV Personality

Unions and Guilds (AFM, ASCAP, BMI, RMA, SAG, etc.)

- Board Member
- Executive Officer
- Office Staff
- Politician

AUTHOR BIOGRAPHIES

ANNIE BOSLER, DMA

Dr. Annie Bosler currently teaches horn at California State University Northridge, Pepperdine University, University of California, Irvine, Pasadena City College, and El Camino College. For nearly ten years she taught at the Colburn School for Performing Arts and also recruited the largest studio within the Winds, Brass, and Percussion Department. She has former horn students in almost every major conservatory across the country. In addition, Annie acted as the horn consultant to actress Shailene Woodley on *The Secret Life of the American Teenager*. Previously holding the title of Colburn School Director of Wellness, Annie travels around the world lecturing about wellness for musicians. Named a TED Educator in 2017, Dr. Bosler co-wrote the viral video *How to practice effectively...for just about anything* and produced and directed the film documentary *1M1: Hollywood Horns of the Golden Years*. As a freelance horn player, Annie has toured with John Williams' *Star Wars in Concert* and with Josh Groban, and performed on *Dancing with the Stars*, *The Ellen Show*, and PBS's *Live from Lincoln Center*, and shared the stage with Ringo Starr and Paul McCartney on CBS's *The Beatles: The Night That Changed America*. She performed with Chance the Rapper at *The Grammy's*, Sean Combs (P-Diddy) at *The American Music Awards*, and Wu-Tang Clan at Coachella. Annie holds a BFA from Carnegie Mellon University where she played varsity tennis, and a MM and DMA from the University of Southern California.

DON GREENE, PhD

Dr. Don Greene, a peak performance psychologist, has taught his comprehensive approach to peak performance mastery at The Juilliard School, Colburn School, New World Symphony, Los Angeles Opera Young Artists Program, Vail Ski School, Perlman Music Program, and US Olympic Training Center. During his thirty-four year career, he has coached more than 1,000 performers to win professional auditions and has guided countless solo performers to successful careers. Some of the performing artists with whom Dr. Greene has worked have won jobs with the Metropolitan Opera Orchestra, New York Philharmonic, Chicago Symphony, San Francisco Opera, Montreal Symphony, Pittsburgh Symphony, National Symphony, Cincinnati Symphony, Pacific Northwest Ballet, and the Dance Theatre of Harlem, to name just a few. Of the Olympic track and field athletes he worked with up until and through the 2016 Games in Rio, 14 won medals, including 5 gold. Dr. Greene has authored eight books including *Audition Success, Fight Your Fear & Win,* and *Performance Success.* In 2017, Dr. Greene was named a TED Educator and collaborated with musician Dr. Annie Bosler to produce the TED-Ed *How to practice effectively...for just about anything.* The video went viral receiving over 25 million views across Facebook and YouTube.

KATHLEEN TESAR, EdD

Dr. Kathleen Tesar has a wide range of experience as both a performer and an administrator in higher education. Currently the Associate Dean for Enrollment Management at The Juilliard School, she oversees the Offices of Admissions and Financial Aid. Her responsibilities include recruiting and enrolling the incoming class each year, overseeing the prescreening and audition processes, chairing the Admissions Committee, and serving on the Scholarship Committee.

Her first job after completing her Bachelor of Music degree at the Eastman School of Music was as a violinist in the Orquesta Sinfonica Municipal in Caracas, Venezuela. Moving back to the U.S., Dr. Tesar spent many years as assistant principal second violin in the Alabama Symphony. As a violin teacher, Dr. Tesar was on the faculty of the Alabama School of Fine Arts and Eastern Music Festival in North Carolina, and maintained a small private studio in Birmingham.

Moving into administration, Dr. Tesar was Director of Admissions first at Eastern Music Festival and then at the Eastman School of Music of the University of Rochester. She worked at the Colburn School for twelve years, her last title as Associate Dean of the Conservatory, and from there went to the University of Southern California Thornton School of Music as Coordinator of the 2016 Piatigorsky International Cello Festival.

In addition to these orchestral and administrative positions, Dr. Tesar was a Fellow at Tanglewood Music Center, and spent several summers as a member of the orchestra at the Spoleto Festival in South Carolina and Italy. She earned her Master of Music degree from the Catholic University of America, and her Doctor of Education (EdD) in Organizational Change and Leadership from the University of Southern California Rossier School of Education. Dr. Tesar's dissertation focused on identifying and recruiting underrepresented students in pre-college classical music programs.